100
YEARS IN PICTURES

HIS MAJESTY KING GEORGE VI

100

YEARS IN PICTURES

A PANORAMA OF HISTORY
IN THE MAKING

WITH TEXT BY

D. C. SOMERVELL

ODHAMS PRESS LIMITED

LONG ACRE, LONDON

1851 QUEEN VICTORIA OPENS THE GREAT EXHIBITION. The world and Victorian Britain were dazzled by the vast exhibition that was opened by the Queen on May Day. Organized under the active patronage of the Prince Consort, it was housed in Paxton's palace of iron and glass covering twenty-six acres and erected in Hyde Park, where it was visited by six million people.

4

Foreword

THE pictures contained in this volume constitute a record of a century in which the human race has changed its habits and its outlook much more rapidly than ever before. One hesitates to call it a century of progress; one need not hesitate to call it a century of acceleration. The pictures, with their captions, tell their own story. Here it is our business to offer some general reflections and an outline which will provide a framework for what follows.

Most people think of the Great Exhibition of 1851 as an entirely new departure and as the invention of Prince Albert. That is not quite accurate. The famous exhibition marked the climax, as it were, of a fashion, and Prince Albert owed much to the activities of a man whose name few now remember, Henry Cole.

In 1846 Cole became a member of the Council of the Society of Arts, then nearly a hundred years old. It is said to have held, in 1756, the very first "exhibition" in Britain and to have set an example followed soon afterwards by the annual exhibitions of the Royal Academy. When Cole joined its Council it, or rather Cole, invited Prince Albert to become its President, for the wedding of art and industry was one of his particular hobbies.

Paris had had industrial exhibitions every five years since Napoleonic days and that of 1844 was admired by numerous English visitors. Inspired by Cole and patronized by Prince Albert, the Society of Arts produced annual exhibitions in its own modest but dignified premises in the years 1847, 1848, 1849 and 1850. But in 1849, while Cole was visiting the Paris exhibition of that year, he conceived something very much bigger and better. Was not the time ripe for London, for England, for the British Empire, to make a new departure and offer hospitality to an *international* exhibition?

Thus was conceived the great idea. Mr. Cole took it to Buckingham Palace and Prince Albert agreed to adopt it. But we must not, in giving Cole his due, push the Prince too far into the background. It was Albert who suggested that a site should be provided for this unprecedentedly gigantic exhibition on the south side of Hyde Park, near where the Albert Memorial now stands. That was at the end of June, 1849.

The site was fixed, but what of the building? As nation after nation accepted the invitation to exhibit its wares it was realized that the building —a temporary building—would have to be ever so much larger than St. Paul's; "as long as Portland Place and three times as wide." The Building Committee invited designs, rejected the hundreds submitted and accepted that of one of their own members, Brunel, the engineer of the Great Western Railway. As soon as Brunel's design was published it was greeted with howls

5

of execration and derision, and a smouldering resentment against the whole grandiose idea leapt into flame. Only at the last moment was Joseph Paxton, the designer of the Duke of Devonshire's gigantic conservatory, brought into the story. He drew a sketch on a piece of blotting paper (still extant in South Kensington), worked out all the details in ten days, submitted it to the committee and published it in the *Illustrated London News*. Opposition quailed and hesitated. Then the editor of *Punch* had a brainwave; he described Paxton's design as "the Crystal Palace." The victory was won. The work was put in hand in July, 1850. The erection of the first and greatest "prefab" was completed within the ten months following. The exhibition was opened on May Day, 1851.

It was a success from the word "go." Six million people paid for admission during its six months' existence, the most assiduous visitors being the Queen and the aged Duke of Wellington, who came roughly three times a week. The net receipts, £356,000, were more than double the whole cost of the show and the profits were devoted to the foundation of the group of permanent exhibitions in South Kensington. When all was over, a Crystal Palace Company was formed to buy the building where it stood and rebuild it in a still more lofty and magnificent form on the top of Sydenham Hill, where it survived until destroyed by fire in 1936.

And now we must cover in a few pages a crowded century of general history.

In 1850 the Queen had been married for ten years, and the seventh of her nine children was born in that year. It was the age of large families. Of course, there had always been a high birth-rate. The peculiarity of the nineteenth century was the fall in the death-rate, particularly infant mortality; most of the brood grew to manhood; hence the unprecedented increase of population.

The year 1850 saw the publication of Tennyson's *In Memoriam* and the elevation of its author to the post of Poet Laureate, which he occupied with unique distinction for over forty years. Next year he rebuked the French for their seventh and revolutionary change of constitution in barely fifty years—"the red fool-fury of the Seine"—and a year later commemorated the death of the Duke of Wellington in a noble ode. *In Memoriam* marks something more than the establishment of Tennyson as the national bard; it symbolizes the deep-seated spiritual unrest of an age distracted by what was called the conflict of religion and science.

Dickens was also at the height of his achievement. *Dombey and Son* (1848) is obsessed by the railway. The working-class suburb where Polly Toodle lives is being bisected by the construction of the first miles of the old London and North-Western Railway. Mr. Dombey's railway journey to Leamington is described with the same gusto that a novelist of, say, 1912 would give to a journey by air, and finally a well-aimed express runs over and abolishes the villain.

The distribution of Britain's population was very different from what it is today. Agriculture still employed two million as compared with just over five million in all forms of industry and commerce. Any hard-and-fast line between rural and urban populations is artificial, but if one applies the same criteria at different dates the results can be instructive. The 1851 census was the first in which "urban" passed ahead of "rural"; by 1881 it was double and today is quadruple.

Trade unions were still in their infancy and confined to certain types of skilled craftsmen who protected themselves by rules of apprenticeship as much against the masses of unskilled labourers below them as against their employers. It is guessed—for there are no statistics—that the total membership of all trade unions was less than 200,000. The engineers' strike of 1852 was the first of any duration and magnitude. Chartism had died down with the advent of the great mid-Victorian prosperity, and the only noticeable socialism was the Christian Socialism of Morris and Kingsley, soon to be reinforced with the eloquence of Ruskin.

Here are some figures for the Londoner. In the 1851 census "the City" reached its maximum population, about 130,000. It was still the home of many a prosperous "City man." By 1901 it had dropped to 26,000 and by 1950 to under 5,000. Those who work there now live elsewhere. A principal agent of the change was the Underground Railway, of which the first

1854 RUSSIAN FORT IN THE CRIMEAN WAR. Nearly forty years of peace were broken for Britain when in March, 1854, she with France declared war on Russia in support of Turkey. Naval and military forces were dispatched to the Crimea, where Sebastopol was stubbornly defended by the enemy until September, 1855. One of their strongest forts was the Redan, shown below.

stretch was opened in 1863. "Tubes" and electrification of the old Underground "Inner Circle" did not come until the beginning of the twentieth century. As for the area now embraced by London County, its population was under a million in 1851 and four and a half million in 1901, from which peak it has since slightly declined. The "Outer Ring" or Suburbia is given as 150,000 in 1851, and just over two million in 1901, and that figure has been doubled since then. Suburbia and the County have now roughly four million each.

Working hours were to us incredibly long, but with the early fifties a notable relaxation began to creep in, the Saturday half-holiday. The railways, at the instigation of Thomas Cook, began running cheap Saturday afternoon excursions. Blackpool was born. But if you had visited Blackpool at that date you would not have seen anyone smoking cigarettes. The cigarette habit was caught by the British soldier from his French allies during the Crimean War (1854–5). The first edition of *Bradshaw* (1840) announced that smoking was forbidden in railway trains *and stations,* but the companies soon began to attach smoking "divans" to their trains. Smoking in the streets was hardly respectable for the respectable classes.

A whole essay might be written on that typically Victorian epithet, "respectable." The essential social process of the age was the steady broadening downwards of "respectability," and the chief agent of the process was, it has been said, *soap.* A "History of Washing" would provide a significant, glorious but perhaps too intimate theme.

Queen Victoria is so often and so stupidly conceived as a prude and a kill-joy that a little evidence to the contrary is desirable. Prince Albert was keenly interested in art and the Queen adopted all his tastes and visited the galleries. In 1853 well-meaning persons warned her against a certain exhibition on account of the prevalence of nudes. She insisted on going, liked them very much and bought one of them. Again, the theatre was at a very low ebb in 1850. Its art was bad and its morals worse; it was not "respectable"; but the Queen had a passion for the stage, insisted on visiting the theatres and ordering "command" performances at Windsor. Things at once began to change for the better and an authoritative historian of the stage says that the change was "probably more due to the action of the Queen than to any general movements in social life."

But the arts all combined counted for much less in 1850 than religion —religious observance in the church, the chapel and the home. "Lord Hatherton used to say," writes G. M. Young, "that in 1810 only two gentlemen in Staffordshire had family prayers; in 1850 only two did not." Volumes of sermons, especially the sermons of Spurgeon of the Metropolitan Tabernacle, whose heyday was considerably later than 1850, were the best-sellers. Among the novelists only Dickens could beat them. The publication of *Hymns Ancient and Modern* in 1861 was an important event, raising the level of the most widespread and popular of the arts. *The English Hymnal* of 1906 was a better book, but it has appealed to a much smaller section of the population.

In 1850 slavery still prevailed in the southern states of the American

1857 EPIC BATTLE IN INDIAN MUTINY. The mutiny of the sepoys of the British Indian Army spread consternation through Britain. The mutineers found no mass support amongst their countrymen, but were able to seize Delhi and besiege Lucknow and other places. Some of the fiercest fighting took place during the recapture of Delhi, particularly at the Cashmere Gate, which is seen above shortly after the battle. The rising was finally suppressed the following year.

9

1860 QUEEN VICTORIA AND HER CONSORT. When this photograph was taken the Queen had been married to Prince Albert of Saxe-Coburg-Gotha for twenty years and was the mother of nine children. Their family life was accepted as a model by most of Britain. Albert, who had been created H.R.H. the Prince Consort in 1857, died of typhoid at Windsor Castle on 14 December, 1861.

1862 PRESIDENT LINCOLN WITH HIS TROOPS. The election of Abraham Lincoln in 1860 as sixteenth President of the U.S.A. was the signal for the Southern States (Confederates) to attempt to secede from the Union and civil war broke out between North and South. Lincoln, the abolitionist, is here seen with his army staff after the Federal victory of Antietam, which turned back Lee's invasion of Northern territory and encouraged Lincoln to issue in the next year his proclamation virtually abolishing slavery throughout the U.S.A.

Union, and the American Government had recently agreed to let Great Britain have the northern half of the vast Pacific territory then called Oregon, where British Columbia was afterwards established. There was no "Dominion of Canada"; that came in 1868. At this date "Canada" meant the provinces of Ontario and Quebec. In Australia, New South Wales had a population of a quarter of a million and all the other colonies together much less. Transportation of convicts to the mainland had been abolished ten years earlier, but still continued to Tasmania. The first rush to Australia followed the discovery of gold there in 1851. In India the last stage of British conquest, the Sikh War, was just over and the Mutiny was seven years ahead.

On the continent of Europe a second Napoleon was about to make himself Emperor of the French. Britons imagined that he would resemble his uncle, and hardly discovered that he did not until the poor man crossed the Channel to end his life as an exile in England twenty years later. There was as yet no German Empire and the Germans were regarded as harmless folk, addicted to philosophy and music. Far the greatest of the continental powers was Russia. Other nations were getting very much alarmed about Russia, for the first but not the last time. The Crimean War was near.

Let us move on to 1875. There have been astonishing changes since 1850. Lincoln and the American Civil War have come and gone, leaving behind them the foundations of the centralized, industrialized U.S.A. of today. American population had overtaken that of Britain in about 1840; now it was far ahead, and the Americans did not like their transatlantic cousins. The key-word of recent Anglo-American relations had been *Alabama,* and England had had to pay £3,000,000 for the depredations of this Confederate ship, which had unfortunately been built in an English shipyard. Garibaldi had come and gone and given his name to a biscuit, and there was a United Italy. In France the "Second Empire" had come and, after the Franco-Prussian War disasters, had gone, leaving behind it an impression of glitter and crinolines and a sort of moral bad smell. In 1875 the French provisional assembly at last adopted its new republican constitution, by a majority of one vote. In Germany, Bismarck had come and—he was still there, ruling until 1890 the empire his genius had clamped together by methods of "blood and iron."

Britain was entering on the last and greatest of the classic struggles between Gladstone and Disraeli, arising out of the conflict between Russia and Turkey. Disraeli, who was Prime Minister, backed the Turks as a bulwark against Russian imperialism. Gladstone, on the other hand, wanted the Turks cleared out "bag and baggage." Disraeli called Gladstone "a sophistical rhetorician inebriated with the exuberance of his own verbosity," and Gladstone replied with the Midlothian campaign. Gladstone won, both at the polls and in the Balkans, but today we rather incline to Disraeli's view. We are more afraid of Stalin than of anyone in Turkey.

Disraeli was the first Prime Minister to make the British Empire ("Empire of England" was what he called it) a substantial plank in his programme. He was also the first Prime Minister to realize that social questions were not secondary matters to be left to junior colleagues. The

1871 PRUSSIA CRUSHES THE SECOND FRENCH EMPIRE. Napoleon III,
nephew of the great Bonaparte was proclaimed emperor in 1852. His
disastrous foreign policy left France with scarcely an ally, and despite a British
offer to act as mediator he plunged into war with Prussia in 1870. The French
Army was numerically stronger and better equipped than the Prussian, but shockingly

12

organized and led. Napoleon with his main army was surrounded and forced to capitulate at Sedan on 2 September, another army was shut up in Metz and the Prussians laid siege to Paris. The capital was valiantly defended, but starvation forced its surrender after four months. This photograph shows Prussian troops in occupation of Fort Issy, one of the ring of forts defending Paris, after its surrender.

13

1885 THE FORTH BRIDGE UNDER CONSTRUCTION. The railway bridge over the Firth of Forth was commenced in 1882 and completed seven years later. The designers adopted the cantilever principle following the collapse of the Tay suspension bridge in 1879. The Forth Bridge is the longest of its type in the world, with spans of 1,710 ft., and is regarded as a notable triumph of bridge-building.

year 1875 saw the first effective statute enabling local authorities to deal with slums.

We pass on to a more cheerful subject, games. The popularity and the organization as spectacles of the great national games are products of great cities and modern transport. The real countryman had his field sports, but he no more needed "games" than a farmer needs to "go for a walk." With modern transport, teams began to play other teams elsewhere, and it then became necessary that they should play according to the same rules. Take football as an example, the most natural and primitive of all games, played with a pig's bladder, gates or the spaces between trees serving as goals, and with perhaps some local feature calling for special rules such as "the wall" at Eton or "the gutter" at Tonbridge. Between 1850 and 1875 nearly all the old local games with their special rules were abandoned. Local diversities crystallized into either "Soccer" (Association), whose rules were drawn up in 1863, or Rugby Union (1871). "International" matches between the four peoples of the United Kingdom began under both sets of rules in the next few years.

In 1875 Dr. W. G. Grace was a young man of twenty-seven. His achievements and his grand personality put cricket on the map as never before. In 1878 an Australian cricket team visited England and started an antipodean rivalry which has continued with increasing seriousness ever since. The county championship system had been started five years earlier. Golf, for centuries the national game of Scotland, gained a foothold at Hoylake near Liverpool in 1869. In 1874 a Major Wingfield patented a game of his own invention under the astonishing title of "sphairistike," which in the course

1900 CANADIANS IN ACTION IN SOUTH AFRICAN WAR. The war against the Boer republics broke out in 1899. Canadian troops served against the Boers and a force is seen above storming a low hill. After a disastrous start, the British under Lord Roberts quickly defeated the main Boer armies and occupied Pretoria, but guerrilla warfare dragged on until 1902.

15

of the next few years was developed, under the guidance of the Marylebone Cricket Club, into lawn tennis. In 1877 the organizers of the game established their headquarters at Wimbledon in partnership with the All-England Croquet Club.

And now we come to 1900. It is the last year of the Queen's reign; she died in the first month of the new century. It was also the central year of the South African War, which seems today a smaller affair than it actually was by the standards of its age. Never before had anything like so large a force been transported to fight on the other side of the world. The war had begun in the previous October in a mood of ridiculous self-confidence, soon to be deflated by the "black week" of December, 1899—Colenso, Stormberg, Magersfontein. On a short view, Britain made a quick recovery and in the

1900 WHITEHALL. This photograph, taken from a spot near where the Cenotaph now stands, emphasizes the enormous changes in the London scene during the past fifty years. The only familiar feature is the traffic jam, caused by street repairs. Although petrol vehicles were legalized by the "Red Flag Act" repeal of 1896, none is visible here. Left is a pile of the wood blocks with which the streets were paved, and a hand-cart is loaded with more of them. Note the gas-lamps which provided lighting; the open-topped horse buses, so pleasant in fine weather and so much the reverse in the wet or cold; the donkey cart, and even the ubiquitous perambulator. There is a general air of leisureliness which contrasts sharply with the breathless haste almost universal nowadays.

16

summer was shouting herself hoarse over the relief of Mafeking. On a long view, it might be said that the deflation of imperialistic grandiosity in "black week" was followed by no subsequent re-inflation. For in spite of Mafeking the war dragged on until it became a bore and a humiliation. Then Joseph Chamberlain called attention to the fact that Britain's world supremacy in commerce and industry was passing and bound to pass. Then Lloyd George stirred up the class war. Then the House of Lords challenged the supremacy of the Commons; the suffragettes challenged the male sex; Dublin and Belfast challenged each other and both challenged Westminster; the miners, the railwaymen and the dockers formed a triple alliance and threatened a general strike; and then came 1914 and the First World War —and the rest. After "black week" nothing ever seemed again to go right

1901 PASSING OF A GREAT QUEEN. Queen
Victoria died 22 January, 1901. Her funeral
cortege is here seen approaching St. George's Chapel,
Windsor, where the funeral ceremony was held.

1909 BLÉRIOT FLIES THE CHANNEL. The Wright brothers had first flown a practical heavier-than-air machine in 1903 and by 1908 flights of over fifty miles had been made. On 29 July, Louis Blériot the Frenchman took off in his monoplane from Calais and thirty-one minutes later crossed, as seen here, the English cliffs near Dover. A new age had dawned.

for Britain for long, though no doubt there is also a brighter side of the picture.

On the last day of February, 1900, when most people were thinking about the relief of Ladysmith, a Labour Representation Committee was created for the promotion of working-class candidatures for parliamentary seats and the establishment of an independent "Labour group" in the House of Commons. All mention of "socialism" was avoided in the prospectus, for it was thought that this notorious word would scare off far more voters than it would attract. Six years later the General Election of 1906, with its great swing to the left, sent thirty Labour members to the new House of Commons. "Working-class" M.P.s had been elected with Liberal support in various suitable constituencies since 1874. Some of them held minor offices in Liberal governments. Keir Hardie had blazed the trail of independent and socialist Labour when he secured election in 1892. The importance

1909 LLOYD GEORGE PRESENTS A NOTABLE BUDGET. The Land Tax proposals of Lloyd George's budget of 1909 led directly to the Parliament Act of 1911. He is here seen clutching the famous dispatch box as he walks to the House of Commons to present his budget. With him are Mrs. Lloyd George and that already rising young politician, Mr. Winston Spencer Churchill.

1913 SUFFRAGETTES AND TRAGEDY AT THE DERBY. Supporters of Mrs. Pankhurst's "Women's Social and Political Union" campaigned for women's suffrage before the First World War. Peaceful methods failing, they tried violence. One of them, Miss Davison, threw herself in front of the King's horse as it rounded Tattenham Corner in the Derby. Horse, jockey and woman (who was killed) are seen, in the picture below, on the ground.

of the Conference of 1900 was that then, for the first time, the trade unions, hitherto non-political, gave their blessing, moral and financial, to the idea of the creation of a new political party.

And if Labour "entered politics" in 1900, so also did Mr. Winston Churchill. Having already seen fighting in three or four continents and trailing clouds of glory from his South African escapade, he was elected a Conservative member for Oldham. He became a Liberal four years later and only returned to the Conservative fold as Chancellor of the Exchequer in 1924.

1900 might be taken to mark the maturity of the bicycle and the infancy of the motor-car. Both meant a return to the road, which had been comparatively deserted during the Victorian railway age. For all sorts of purposes, business and pleasure, bicycles enlarged the horizon of ordinary people who could not afford horses and carriages. The car which, with the motor-coach and the lorry, was to drive the railways near bankruptcy was not, like the railway, a British invention. The internal-combustion engine was patented by a German, and the first practicable cars were built in France and Germany. The notorious Red Flag Act, which made motoring impossible on English roads, was repealed in 1896 and the event was celebrated by a processional expedition from London to Brighton. From the car to the aeroplane is but a short step. The Wright brothers first flew a heavier-than-air machine in 1903. Blériot flew the Channel in 1909, and two Englishmen, Alcock and Brown, flew directly across the Atlantic in 1919.

The same year (1896) that legalized the motor-car saw the establishment of Harmsworth's *Daily Mail,* followed in 1900 by Pearson's *Daily Express,* and in 1903 by Harmsworth's *Daily Mirror,* a picture paper suitable for such as found reading difficult and intended, as its name artfully suggested, mainly for women. Harmsworth got his idea from the weekly *Tit-bits* on which he had been employed in his youth, and the new democratic journalism "titbitized" the news. On this topic gloomy sermons have been preached, but the revolution had its good side and its influence extended far beyond the new halfpenny Press. Even *The Times* was titbitized up to a point. A copy of the Victorian *Times* would strike the most earnest of modern readers as intolerably stodgy.

Sabbatarianism was in retreat, and in 1896 the public museums and galleries were for the first time thrown open on Sundays. But if religion was a declining force, art, and more particularly music, was gaining ground. Somewhere near the beginning of Victoria's reign Carlyle had described the British as a dumb nation, "our only Mozart Sir Henry Bishop" —and Sir Henry was the composer of *Home, Sweet Home.* The Gilbert and Sullivan operas, first-class works within their own limits, and perhaps the only products of the Victorian imagination which have suffered no diminution of popularity, fall within the fifteen years 1875–90. Parry and Stanford raised the level of more serious British music, and at exactly the turn of the century a brighter star, one of the great masters of modern orchestra, rose above the horizon. Elgar's *Enigma Variations* appeared in

1899 and *The Dream of Gerontius* in 1900, though it is significant that the latter received its first adequate performance in Germany.

In 1895 Henry Wood conducted, in the newly opened Queen's Hall, London, the first of his fifty series of autumnal Promenade Concerts, evening orchestral concerts at popular prices every night for about nine weeks. A rising standard of popular taste is suggested by comparing the programmes of the earlier series with those of the later ones.

The gramophone already existed in 1900, but for some years tone-quality was good enough for nothing more exalted than a comic song.

1915 FIRST WORLD WAR. Within a few months of the outbreak of war, the combatants in the west had pinned each other down on a line stretching from the Swiss frontier to the English Channel at Dixmude. Along a front of some 400 miles millions of men went to earth in a vast system of trenches, where the defensive power of the machine-gun reigned supreme. Since neither side could outflank the other, they tried alternately to break through their opponent's defences in a series of murderous battles on a titanic scale—Verdun, Ypres, the Somme, Passchendaele were the main battlegrounds—in which the flower of the youth of western Europe was butchered. This scene of British casualties on the Ypres-Menin road, walking or awaiting clearance to a dressing station, portrays vividly the suffering and the misery which, for four and a quarter years, were the daily lot of the fighting troops of many different nations on the Western Front.

In U.S.A., Theodore Roosevelt was about to become President. Most great men achieve greatness by dealing with a great crisis. Washington, Lincoln and Roosevelt II are obvious examples among American presidents. Roosevelt I performed the more difficult feat of becoming a great man in what was, comparatively, a dead calm. He put his country "on the map" as a World Power as no American had done before. In 1890 most Englishmen had difficulty in recalling the name of the American President. In 1904 he was clearly one of the two most conspicuous figures in the world.

The other was the German Kaiser, who had just begun building a fleet

1917 LENIN SPEAKS. Russia was the first of the combatants to go under in the First World War. The Tsarist régime cracked under the double strain of military disaster and rising popular discontent. After a period of confusion the most militant section of the revolutionaries, the Bolsheviks, led by Lenin, seized power in October, 1917. Until then unknown to the world at large, Lenin organized the lightning stroke which ousted the moderate Kerensky. It was Lenin whose utter ruthlessness consolidated Bolshevik power; and it was he whose genius laid the foundation of the tremendous machine which, by the middle of the twentieth century, had brought Russia to the position of one of the two leading world powers. He is here seen addressing a crowd in Petrograd.

designed to rival the British. The long Victorian security was about to end. In 1904 the *Entente Cordiale* (not quite an alliance) with France was established. This was very much a new departure in British policy. Only six years earlier we had seemed to be not far from war with France over rival claims to the Upper Nile—Fashoda was the point of collision.

Russia was aggressive in the Far East and Japan was preparing to contest her claims. The Anglo-Japanese Alliance of 1902 strengthened her hands—and strengthened those of Britain by enabling her to withdraw most of her Pacific fleet to home waters.

In 1900 the "colonies" of Australia were federated in a single Commonwealth. The Dominion of Canada had since 1885 enjoyed the unifying influence of the Canadian Pacific Railway and the consequent development of the wheatfields of its prairie provinces. In India Lord Curzon was enthroned, the last of the great Viceroys of the old order. Indian "unrest" and Indian "reforms" were about to begin, and to lead, in less than half a century, to Indian independence.

When we reach 1925 we seem to have crossed a great gulf. 1900 was still Victorian: 1925 is modern. By 1925 the First World War was a memory. Despite the efforts of Edward the Peacemaker and the scepticism of the vast majority, war had come to Europe in 1914 and rapidly spread over the entire globe. It was a titanic struggle, the first of the totalitarian as opposed to dynastic wars. In its result it left a trail of desolation, moral and material. It altered the face of Europe almost beyond recognition and, what is more, through producing the Russian Revolution, changed the political allegiances of the peoples who inhabit one-quarter of the land surface of the globe.

1926 BRITAIN FACES A GENERAL STRIKE. After nine months of crisis the coal-miners refused to accept a reduction in wages and came out on 1 May. The T.U.C. ordered on 4 May a sympathetic strike of railwaymen, transport workers and printers. This "General Strike" collapsed after nine days. Ugly incidents occurred between strikers and volunteers operating transport and other services. Here a burnt-out bus is being towed away after a clash at the Elephant and Castle, London, watched by strikers and members of the public. The Elephant and Walworth Road were frequently the scene of incidents such as this.

1936 NAZI RALLY AT NUREMBERG. Vast and theatrically staged rallies were
a feature of the Nazi party's rise and were continued after Hitler was
made Chancellor in 1933. This one was staged to permit Hitler, accompanied by
Himmler and Lutze, to pay tribute to Germany's dead in the First World War.

1938 CHAMBERLAIN RETURNS FROM MUNICH. After his rape of Austria Hitler turned on Czechoslovakia, demanding the cession of territory to protect the German minorities. France was bound to the Czechs by treaty and Britain to France. War seemed certain. At the last moment Hitler agreed to a meeting at Munich and peace was preserved at the price of Czechoslovakia's dismemberment. The British Premier is seen on his return reading the famous "piece of paper" signed by Hitler which Chamberlain accepted as a "No More War" pledge.

Neither the Treaty of Versailles which ended the war, nor the League of Nations which grew out of it, achieved the end of putting the Humpty-Dumpty world together again. The Russian Revolution overthrew an old-fashioned despotism to establish in its place an efficient, ruthless dictatorship; but it did more. It put Communism, hitherto a text-book political theory, on the map of reality. In its new position, Communism proved an attraction outside Russia for millions who found that non-Communist types of society were unable to provide them with all the things they thought they deserved.

In the years before 1914 the key-note of the world was stability. By 1925 it was clear that the new key-note was fluidity. The German, the Russian and the Austro-Hungarian Empires had fallen, and the British Empire, though still strong and unified, was showing signs of strain. In Britain, the Russian Revolution had produced a marked political swing to the

left and the first Labour Government (a minority government) had taken office. Perhaps it was still rather too young for such responsibilities. The nine-months' Labour Government of 1924 achieved a resounding success in Anglo-Franco-German relations. The fact that Ramsay MacDonald's London Agreement proved a false dawn does not alter the fact that it looked like a dawn at the time. Thereafter, however, the Labour Government collapsed largely over the ridiculous Campbell prosecution affair. So Baldwin came back into office, and his Foreign Secretary, Austen Chamberlain, carried on the good work of MacDonald by negotiating the Locarno Treaty, 1925. Hitler had emerged from a brief imprisonment and was putting the finishing touches to *Mein Kampf*.

What most concerned the Western world in 1925 was not the German menace but the General Strike menace in Britain, not A. Hitler, but A. J. Cook, who described himself as "a humble disciple of Lenin." The General Strike might have come in July, 1925. Baldwin secured its postponement until May, 1926. The subject still arouses partisan passions.

One fact about the General Strike is beyond controversy. It gave broadcasting the best advertisement it ever received. Wireless telegraphy by

1944 D-DAY. The Second World War broke out in September, 1939, with Hitler's attack on Poland. By 1944 almost every country in the world was involved. France had fallen in 1940; Europe was over-run. On 6 June, 1944, the Allies landed on beach-heads in Normandy. On the left, British troops are seen wading ashore, with some of the specially built tank-landing craft lying off the beaches.

1945 YALTA CONFERENCE. The Allies' "Big Three," Churchill, Roosevelt and Stalin, had met at Teheran in 1943 when the tide was on the turn. They met again at Yalta in February, 1945, when the war with Germany was clearly nearing its close. Amongst decisions taken was that to hold the San Francisco conference from which grew up the United Nations Organization. Below, the three leaders are seen with members of their staffs. Roosevelt, a sick man then, died less than two months later.

"dots and dashes" dates from the first year of the new century, when Marconi sent his first wireless messages across the Atlantic. Wireless telephony followed, and broadcasting as we understand it today was first used in the American presidential election of 1920. By 1926 quite a number of folk in Britain had radio sets, but a much larger number had not. The General Strike included a strike of printers and suddenly deprived people of their newspapers. So they trooped round to neighbours' houses to hear the news and came home determined to get one of these machines themselves. The year 1925 represents about the same stage in tele-audition as 1950 represents in television.

From the wireless it seems natural to pass to the motion picture. In the primitive form of the kinetoscope it was launched by the American Edison, who invented so many things, in 1894. In the first years of the century you could see what would now be called a "documentary" entitled *Our Navy* at the London Polytechnic. The use of the screen for fictional drama came later, and, incredible as it may appear, the actors and actresses remained anonymous, though not for long. Charlie Chaplin conquered Britain during the First World War. The first "talkies" date from 1928.

Fourteen years after 1900 came the First World War. Fourteen years after 1925 came the Second. What we call nowadays the inter-war period may be divided into post-war I and pre-war II, the first a period in which the world seemed to be recovering from the first war, and the other one in which it was drifting towards the second. Where does the dividing line lie? It is to be found in that devastating event, the Great Slump, which began with the collapse of the American stock market in 1929 and deepened for three or four years following. In Great Britain it broke the second Labour Government. In America it led to Franklin Roosevelt and the New Deal. In Germany it led straight to Hitler. There will perhaps always be controversy, there has certainly been a great deal of misrepresentation, of the part played by Baldwin and Neville Chamberlain in guiding Britain through the years which followed the establishment of Nazi rule in Germany. There is no controversy about the part played by Churchill, and when the first crisis of the Second World War broke over Great Britain he was there to take charge.

In 1939 the unstable Europe of the Versailles Treaty collapsed again. By 1945 Europe was in ruins, literally and metaphorically, and the whole balance of pre-war power politics had altered. There were but two world powers left, the U.S.A. and the U.S.S.R., though the British Empire still held together. At its conclusion, the political left-wing had triumphed in nearly every country. In Britain, Labour went into office with an overwhelming majority and the scene was set for a period of five years of social experiment and democratic revolution that rivals in significance the Industrial Revolution. But the problems of a shattered world were not to be solved by hope and fervour; strange wartime alliances could not be cemented by speeches. Within a year or so the Iron Curtain had made its ominous appearance, and the United Nations, which had replaced the moribund League of Nations, looked itself almost as moribund. In Britain, recovery

1945 VE-DAY IN LONDON. Germany surrendered unconditionally to the Allies on 7 May. The following day was dedicated to Victory in Europe. Above, the King and Queen, with the two princesses and the Premier, Winston Churchill, greet the enthusiastic London crowd from Buckingham Palace balcony.

1945 FIRST ATOM BOMB. In the morning of 6 August a U.S.A. aircraft dropped an atomic bomb on Hiroshima, Japan. Four square miles of the city were destroyed and nearly 200,000 people killed and injured. A new and terrifying future opened before humanity. Left is seen the vast cloud flung into the sky immediately after the explosion of the bomb.

from war damage and disaster was slow and painful. Only America's generosity succeeded in bridging the Dollar Gap.

By 1950 there was some reaction. A swing to the right had been noticeable, particularly in France, Italy and the part of Germany occupied by the Western Powers. In the 1950 British Election the huge Labour majority melted overnight. The Labour Party secured a slender majority and continued in office, but the political future was studded with question marks.

Some historians profess to find evidence that the second half of each century is a time of expansion and progress, while the first half is fraught with difficulty, danger and often disaster. The year 1851 ushered in fifty years of astonishing strength and solidity which, for all its mistakes, did achieve great progress. The year 1900 saw a world in decline while its technical abilities increased a thousandfold. Now 1951 brings us—what?

1950 STATE OPENING OF A NEW PARLIAMENT. The General Election in Britain in February swept away the Labour Government's huge majority and produced a condition of near stalemate. The new House of Commons met on 6 March, and here the King and Queen are seen in the state coach leaving Buckingham Palace on their way to the Palace of Westminster to open Parliament.

A century in pictures

THE pictures in the following pages provide a pictorial record of one of the most eventful centuries in history. They are not, however, designed to provide a connected sequence of historical events, though events play their part. Rather, they are designed as a visual commentary upon the changing scene as well as the unfolding drama of history. Wherever appropriate, contemporary prints have been used, but on the whole photographs, the records of the impartial lens of the camera, have been preferred.

1850 LONDON'S OXFORD CIRCUS. The picture above shows the crossing of Oxford Street and Regent Street, at Oxford Circus. The view looks down Upper Regent Street. That street was designed by John Nash to connect a never-built villa of the Prince Regent with his old residence of Carlton House. Nash's buildings have disappeared today, but his beautiful layout of Regent Street remains.

1851 BANK OF ENGLAND AND ROYAL EXCHANGE, LONDON. This leisurely
scene is representative of even the heart of the City in the middle of the
nineteenth century. The building on the right is the third Royal Exchange on this
site, replacing that which was burned to the ground in 1838. On the left is the

Bank of England, founded to help finance the war with Louis XIV at the end of the seventeenth century. The premises shown here were designed by George Sampson in 1734 as its permanent quarters, and were extensively altered and enlarged by Sir John Soane fifty years later. For safety, there were no external windows.

1851 CRYSTAL PALACE IN HYDE PARK. When all other designs for a building to house the 1851 Great Exhibition had failed to satisfy the Exhibition Committee, Joseph Paxton sketched on a piece of blotting paper his scheme for implementing Brunel's design. The result was the building shown right, differing in important respects, it will be noted, from the modified form in which it was later re-erected at Sydenham. During the six months of its employment as an exhibition building it was visited by more than six million people from all over the world—an unprecedented achievement which entailed a net profit of £213,000.

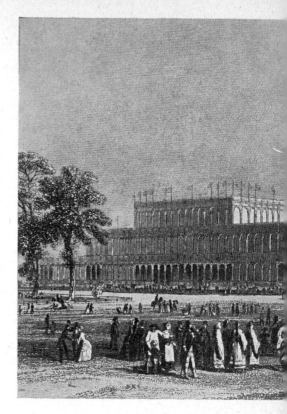

1851 CRICKET AT TONBRIDGE SCHOOL. This painting by C. Tattershall Dodd, drawing master at Tonbridge School in 1851, depicts a match on "The Head," as the school match ground is still called. The school was founded in 1553 by an ex-Lord Mayor of London, Sir Andrew Judd, and endowed by the Skinners' Company. The buildings shown in the painting no longer exist, the school having been rebuilt in 1865. The school's interest in cricket has, however, continued unabated. For many a year now the annual match against Clifton has been held at Lord's ground, St. Marylebone, thus conferring on Tonbridge cricketers the proud distinction of being numbered among the six so-called "Lord's schools."

37

1852 FUNERAL OF THE DUKE OF WELLINGTON. The "Iron Duke," eighty-three years old at his death, forms a notable link between two eras. Thirty-seven years earlier he had finally crushed Napoleon. In 1942 his godson, Field-Marshal the Duke of Connaught, died during the Second World War.

1852 NEW HOUSES OF PARLIAMENT. The old Palace of Westminster was burned down in 1834. A parliamentary committee was appointed to supervise its rebuilding. The edifice shown here, in the "Gothic revival" style, was erected to the plans of Sir Charles Barry and opened by Queen Victoria in 1852.

1852 NAPOLEON III TAKES TITLE OF "EMPEROR." Born in 1808, nephew of the great Bonaparte, Prince Louis Napoleon, shown right, conceived that the Bonaparte dynasty was destined to be revived in his person. For the sake of his "destiny" he wrote pamphlets, made hopeless insurrections, endured imprisonment. His opportunity came with the French democratic-socialist revolution of 1848. Elected president of the "Second Republic," he converted his presidency into a dictatorship in 1851 and assumed the imperial title the following year.

1853 PERRY OPENS UP JAPAN. In 1636, alarmed by the spread of European influences, Japan shut herself up from the rest of the world and became a "hermit nation." By mid-nineteenth century European expansion had made inevitable the opening up of Japan, which was accomplished by the American Commodore Perry. On 8 July, 1853, he entered Uraga Harbour with four warships, bearing a letter from the U.S. President "requesting" the conclusion of a commercial treaty.

1853 NEW TOWNS "DOWN UNDER." Britain was developing important settlements in the Southern Continent. New Zealand had been annexed in 1840
to forestall the French, believed to be on the point of taking possession. The capital
was fixed at Auckland, shown above as it was thirteen years later, including the
famous windmill which is still extant in a city of more than 250,000 people. Meanwhile
Melbourne, called after Queen Victoria's first Prime Minister, had been founded
in 1841. The illustration below shows the first Town Hall with its tower, somewhat
overshadowing the city's first Court House, which is visible to the left of the picture.

Today, Melbourne is a thriving modern city of some 1,200,000 inhabitants.

1854 OPENING OF THE CRYSTAL PALACE, SYDENHAM. Queen Victoria's interest in the Crystal Palace continued after the modified building was removed to Sydenham. Here the Queen and the Prince Consort, the Emperor Napoleon III and the Empress Eugénie are seen at its opening. The Palace became a centre for the popularization of classical music and notable for its gigantic Handel festivals.

1855 STEAM CARRIAGE ON THE ROADS. Trevithick devised a steam carriage which ran successfully on roads as early as 1801, and he had several successful imitators. This illustration shows a road carriage intended for private use. The development of such vehicles was blocked by an Act of Parliament in 1865 which restricted their speed to 4 m.p.h. on country roads and to 2 m.p.h. in towns. The Act was not repealed until 1896.

41

1855 WAR IN THE CRIMEA. Hostilities with Russia broke out in 1854, Britain and France aiding Turkey against the encroachments of Russia in the Near East. The Allies' main undertaking was the siege of the Russian Black Sea port of Sebastopol, in the Crimean Peninsula. The siege was brought to a successful conclusion after almost exactly a year, and the battles whose names still adorn ugly little groups of cottages in various parts of Britain—Alma, Balaklava, Inkerman—were all incidental to that chief objective. These brilliant early photographs by Roger Fenton show, respectively, the cook-house of the 8th Hussars and, below, a quiet moment in a mortar battery. The day of the "action photograph" had not yet dawned, but one can admire the surprising results which this early war photographer achieved with his primitive apparatus.

1855 FLORENCE NIGHTINGALE, A GREAT PIONEER. Born into the highest
social circles, Miss Nightingale revolutionized British hospital organization
during the Crimean War. During the next thirty years, in face of bitter prejudice, she
established nursing as a profession for educated women on a basis both honourable
and efficient. In 1907 she became the first woman recipient of the O.M.

1856 AWARDS FOR CRIMEAN HEROES. In 1856 Queen Victoria instituted the Victoria Cross as the highest British award for valour in the face of an enemy. She is here seen on the Horse Guards Parade distributing awards to heroes of

44

the war in the Crimea, lately brought to an end. The new V.C. may well have been the guerdon of a very few much-envied recipients on this occasion. This award carries a small pension and takes precedence over all other medals or orders.

1857 SIR ISAMBARD KING-DOM BRUNEL (1806-1859) was the son of an equally eminent father. I. K. Brunel designed the "Great Western," one of the earliest steamships to cross the Atlantic, and the "Great Eastern," which was the largest ship built within the nineteenth century. He built the Clifton Suspension Bridge and, in addition, was Chief Engineer of the Great Western Railway.

1857 THE BRITISH ROYAL FAMILY. In order of seniority, the children shown in this photograph, the original of which is at Windsor Castle, include "Vicky," married the following year to the Crown Prince of Prussia, and mother of Kaiser Wilhelm II; "Bertie," afterwards Edward VII; Alice, who became great-grandmother of the Duke of Edinburgh; Alfred; Helena; Louise; Arthur (Duke of Connaught); Leopold; Beatrice.

1857 SIR COLIN CAMPBELL, afterwards Lord Clyde (1792-1863). As a young man he served throughout the Peninsular War. In the Crimea he was mainly responsible for the victory of the Alma and the British "thin red line" at Balaklava. Upon the outbreak of the Indian Mutiny, he became Commander-in-Chief in India.

1857-58 SCENES FROM THE INDIAN MUTINY. The outbreak of the Indian Mutiny came as a profound shock to the people at home in Britain. For that very reason they were the more stirred by the acts of heroism performed during the overthrow of the mutineers. These pictures show three notable incidents. Above is depicted the storming of Delhi's Cashmere Gate. Captured by the rebels in May, 1857, Delhi was the chief centre of rebellion. It was retaken in September after days of hard fighting. Top right is a reproduction of Goodall's famous picture, "The Campbells are Coming." Europeans and loyal sepoys defended numerous women and children in the Lucknow Residency until Sir Henry Havelock burst through with a small relieving force, to be besieged in his turn for many weeks. At the most anxious stage of this second siege a Scots girl leaped upon the walls and declared that she heard the swirl of far-distant bagpipes. "The Cam'ells are comin'," she cried. She was right. Lucknow was finally relieved by Sir Colin Campbell on 16 November, and the illustration on the right shows the scene when Havelock and Campbell met.

48

1858 "DERBY DAY," BY FRITH. The enormous panoramic pictures of William Frith (1819-1909) were immensely popular in their own day. Although subject to perhaps undeserved disparagement by many critics, they have a special value for us as recording the contemporary scene faithfully and in great detail. At the time of its exhibition at the Royal Academy, the Derby Day canvas was condemned by the pre-Raphaelites on account of the "vulgarity" of its subject. We, on the other hand, are grateful to the artist for his realistic portrayal of all classes of mid-Victorian society as they foregathered in their thousands on Epsom Downs.

1858 FRITH'S "RAMSGATE SANDS." Painted and exhibited a few years earlier than the picture above, "Ramsgate Sands" was criticized on its exhibition because, said the critics, it contained no grateful mother nursing a convalescent child! Nevertheless, it was purchased by Queen Victoria, and it remains a valuable record of the customs and costumes of an age when men and women in Britain were only beginning to appreciate the merits of a seaside holiday. It seems quite safe to assume that even such seaside "creations" as those shown on page 178 were a conception which cannot have entered the most daring or imaginative of minds for many years to come.

51

1859 BLONDIN CROSSING THE NIAGARA FALLS. Charles Blondin (1824-97), a Frenchman, was the most famous rope-walker of all time. This remarkable photograph shows him crossing Niagara in 1859. A week later he repeated the feat blindfold and wheeling a barrow; six weeks later carrying a man on his back; and in 1860 on stilts, in the presence of the Prince of Wales.

1860 LORD PALMERSTON ADDRESSES THE HOUSE. In January, 1855, at the critical period of the Crimean War, Palmerston became Prime Minister at the age of seventy. He held office for most of the next ten years, dying in harness. In his last ministry (1859-65) he was joined by the "Peelites," including Gladstone, who is seen above making notes while his chief speaks.

1860 THE LAST BARE-KNUCKLE FIGHT. The golden age of prize-fighting ended with the Regency, the Sayers v. Heenan contest, shown below, thirty years later being a last revival of a brave tradition. The contest between the English David, Tom Sayers, and the American Goliath, Heenan, was technically illegal, and was eventually stopped by the police.

1860 LAST OF THE GREAT THREE-DECKERS: H.M.S. "VICTORIA." At about 1860 three fundamental changes were gradually revolutionizing the British Navy: from sail to steam; from wood to ironclad hull; from internal broadside fire to external centre-line guns. The "Victoria," "the last and finest of British three-deckers," was obsolete before completion and served only one commission.

1860 MEETING OF VICTOR EMMANUEL AND GARIBALDI.
In May, 1860, Garibaldi commenced his sensationally successful assault on the Bourbon Kingdom of Sicily and Naples, on behalf of King Victor Emmanuel, who brought his regular army down the "leg" of Italy as the red-shirt leader ascended it. They met, as shown here, midway between Rome and Naples.

1861 ALEXANDER THE LIBERATOR OF RUSSIA. Tsar from 1855 to 1881, Alexander was the most liberal-minded of Russian rulers. In 1861 he emancipated 23,000,000 serfs in his realm, only to die at the hand of an assassin twenty years later.

1861-65 AMERICAN CIVIL WAR. The print reproduced above, showing negro ex-slaves parading with the liberation manifesto, depicts a scene so characteristic and so impressed upon the modern mind that we are in danger of forgetting what this four-year struggle was about. The inauguration of Abraham Lincoln as President of the United States in 1861 caused opinion in the eleven "Southern" States to fear that, with his well-known abolitionist views, he would end the system of slave labour on which their economy was based. They, therefore, broke away from the Union to form a "Confederacy" of their own, and the so-called civil war was in fact the successful attempt of the "Federal" northerners to reconquer the South. From the first the latter were clearly overweighted in both economic resources and manpower, being able to muster only some 650,000 men to the Federalists' 2,500,000. The incident which really marked the opening of the war was the Confederates' capture of Fort Sumter, in Charleston Harbour, on 13 April, 1861. The first battle was fought on 21 July, when advancing northerners under McDowell were defeated at Bull Run. However, the Federal resources were bound to tell. The area now known as West Virginia was speedily conquered and brought into the Union. A new army under McClellan was formed and trained in the neighbourhood of Washington. After this it was a question of time. Aided by McClellan's lack of enterprise and the skill of their General Lee the South resisted gallantly and had many individual successes, notably those gained by "Stonewall" Jackson. But the North soon discovered in Grant a most able general of their own. Appointed in 1864 to the supreme command of the Union armies, he gradually wore down his opponents. Lee surrendered to him on 9 April, 1865, and resistance was virtually over.

1862 CIVIL WAR HIGHLIGHTS. The struggle in America was notable for many things, among them the first fight between ironclad warships, portrayed above in a contemporary print. This took place at Hampton Roads, Virginia, between the Federal "Monitor," whose turret is plainly seen, and the Confederate "Merrimac." Neither suffered vital damage. The picture below of a Federal gun and its crew is a fine example of the work of Matthew Brady who, with Britain's Roger Fenton, shares the distinction of pioneering the work of the camera in war.

1862 UNION ARTILLERY AT YORKTOWN. McClellan, the Union commander-in-chief, made Yorktown, on the coast of Virginia, the base for his "Peninsular campaign." This was an attempt to attack the Southern capital of Richmond by ferrying an army round the coast. The Brady photograph above shows McClellan's artillery park, with a pile of round cannon-balls, not yet superseded by the shell.

1862 FIRST LONDON TRAMS. Confronted with the experience of some large provincial towns and of Paris, London probably showed wisdom in being slow to adopt trams. Here the first Metropolitan horse trams are shown at Marble Arch. Less handy than buses, they greatly obstructed other forms of traffic.

1863 GLADSTONE OPENS THE METROPOLITAN RAILWAY. London's first underground railway, the "Met" from Baker Street to the City, was opened by Gladstone, here seen with other notables in the nearest truck. It was soon followed by the District Railway, and the two were then joined to form the Inner Circle.

1863 VICTORIANS AT HOME. These obviously posed family groups of upper-middle-class Victorians epitomize both the stiffness of contemporary family life and the patriarchal authority of the husband and father. At the same time, these were men of real attainments and enlightenment. The Rev. Thomas Guthrie, left, was a minister of the Scottish Church, and a notable reformer whose chief interests were the Ragged Schools and temperance. His books on these themes enjoyed an enormous sale. Dr. Worsley, seen below with his wife in their drawing-room at Downing College, Cambridge, was also a man of mark. It was a common and sensible practice of well-to-do Victorians to be photographed, not in a professional studio but in their own natural environment, at home.

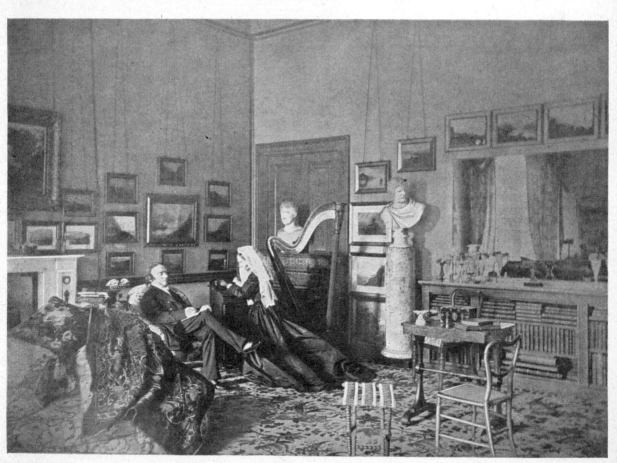

1863 BY THE SEASIDE. Victorian holiday-makers, as the picture above shows, tended to take their pleasures primly. Seaside holidays had caught on rapidly by this date and resorts like Ramsgate (see pages 50-51), Margate and other places were becoming increasingly popular with the so-called "working classes." Fashionable society was tending to turn towards quieter and more "select" resorts and many unknown fishing villages (such as Swanage seen here) were coming into prominence.

1863 SARAH BERNHARDT. Probably the most famous actress of her century, Bernhardt was born in 1844 of a French father and a German mother. At the date of this photograph she was still only a young girl, but was already famous, and was still acting in the early years of the twentieth century. The "Divine Sarah" died in 1923.

1864 PRUSSO-DANISH WAR: FORT DUPPEL. This war marked the beginning of Prussia's ascendancy in Central Europe. The "Schleswig-Holstein question" had long been complex. Bismarck's Prussia determined to settle it by force of arms and, in a brief campaign, seized the Duchies which for several centuries had belonged to the Danish crown. The Danes were crushed at Fort Duppel, seen above heavily damaged by enemy gunfire, after a brief but valiant resistance.

1864 MID-VICTORIAN SPORT IN ENGLAND. Croquet seems to have been brought from France to Ireland and thence to England, where it arrived in 1856. An all-England tournament was organized at Wimbledon in 1868, a few years after the date of the top picture, which represents a typical croquet party. Cricket was on the threshold of its golden age, "W.G." having just entered the lists at the age of sixteen. An elementary county championship, arranged in 1864, was won by Surrey, and such local teams as that shown below were to be found throughout the country.

1865 ABRAHAM LINCOLN ASSASSINATED. Born in 1809, son of a Kentucky farmer, Abraham Lincoln spent his early life in the backwoods. He was elected to the Illinois legislature in 1834, studied law in his spare time and began to practise in 1837. From this point may be dated his rise as an orator of world class. Elected to Congress for a two-year term in 1847, by 1858, when he stood for the Senate, he was a national figure. In 1860 he was elected President. Re-elected in 1864, he was by now a statesman of world stature. He was shot dead by John Wilkes Booth, an actor, four months later, shortly after the above photograph was taken. The poster here reproduced indicates the fabulous sums offered for the murderer's apprehension. Booth was caught and shot soon after.

1865 SCENES FROM THE ENGINEERING INDUSTRY. In 1828 the charter of the "Institution of Civil Engineers" (London) had included in civil engineering "the construction and adaptation of machinery." With the progress of industrial developments there was soon scope for a separate "Institution of Mechanical Engineers," founded at Birmingham in 1847 with George Stephenson as its first president. Large engineering works sprang up all over the country, these illustrations showing Penn and Sons' works, above, at Greenwich, and Rennies' works at Deptford, two which were at this time typical of many others. To modern eyes the managerial group in the lower picture may seem unsuitably clad, but less formal clothes would have been unthinkable in the minds of their wearers.

1866 "GREAT EASTERN" COMPLETES THE ATLANTIC CABLE. This ship, designed by I. K. Brunel and launched in 1858, was a premature monster, 680 ft. long, with a gross tonnage of 18,915. Fitted with both screw and paddles, she was hopelessly under-powered, and her dimensions were not attempted again until the "Oceanic" of 1899. However, her vast storage capacity made her the only vessel afloat which could carry the whole of the 2,500 miles of the Atlantic submarine cable. After several abortive efforts to lay a satisfactory cable with two ships, the "Great Eastern" alone made the attempt in 1865. As so often before, the cable fractured and sank, but a final venture the next year was successful. On 28 July, 1866, the western end, having been spliced to the main cable, was landed at Heart's Content, Newfoundland.

1866 AUSTRO-PRUSSIAN WAR: BATTLE OF KONIGGRATZ. The second step in Prussia's advance towards Central European domination quickly followed the first (see page 62). The occupation of Schleswig-Holstein jointly by the Austrians and Prussians soon led to war between them. The conflict, which from the first hostilities to the armistice lasted less than six weeks, has been called the only perfect example of "Blitzkrieg," or lightning war. This contemporary print, so typical of "battle scenes" of those days, shows the Emperor Francis Joseph of Austria on the field of Koniggratz (or Sadowa), at which, despite these appearances, the Austrians were crushingly defeated, and the war ended in Prussia's favour. As a result, a North German Confederation was created which was under the effective control of Prussia.

1866 RIOTING IN HYDE PARK. A demonstration in favour of Lord John Russell's defeated Reform Bill was staged for 23 July at Hyde Park. The authorities closed the park for the day, whereupon the demonstrators pulled down 1,400 ft. of the park railings.

1867 FENIAN OUTRAGE. The "Fenian" movement was brought to Ireland by disbanded soldiers of the American Civil War. In September, 1866, two Fenians arrested at Manchester were rescued from a prison van, as shown here, and a policeman was killed.

1867 TRAGEDY OF AN "EMPEROR." One of the minor international events that profoundly shook the nineteenth-century world was the Mexican adventure of Napoleon III and the Hapsburg Archduke Maximilian. Mexico in the early sixties was under the control of a dictator, Benito Juarez, who had seized power by force, and in the contemporary photograph below his troops are seen making formal entry into Mexico City. His opponents, the Catholic Conservatives, were largely in exile and Napoleon III of France thought this a heaven-sent opportunity to extend French influence by sending an expedition to overthrow the dictatorship. He expanded this into a scheme for a "Latin Empire" of which the Archduke Maximilian was persuaded to become Emperor. But the expedition was badly handled; Mexicans, whatever their internal grievances, united against foreign interference; and finally the U.S., relieved of its Civil War preoccupations, vigorously reasserted the Monroe doctrine. The French withdrew. Maximilian, perhaps quixotically, refused to desert "his people," was betrayed and shot at Queretaro on 19 June, 1867. Juarez then resumed the dictatorship until his death in 1872.

1867 FEDERATION OF CANADA. The problems arising in Canada out of the existence of many independent provinces resulted in acute political and economic difficulties. The obvious solution was federation and, after preliminary conferences, the statesmen involved moved to London, where they are seen (top left) in session. The British North America Act, 1867, was passed and brought the Dominion of Canada into being.

1867 SAIL AND STEAM. By this date steam as a motive power was revolutionizing transport by land and sea, but by an irony of fate it was about this period that the finest and loveliest sailing ships ever built were active. Below, left, are seen in Calcutta harbour some of the beautiful clippers that plied the Far Eastern routes in the sixties. They were doomed to extinction. Below, right, is a contemporary scene at Waterloo Station, London. The locomotive looks strangely old-fashioned to modern eyes, but it and its fellows were already astonishingly efficient and were pulling ever larger trains at high average speeds over tracks which by this date had reached a mileage of 115,000 in Britain.

1868 EMPIRE CONTRAST. By this time the city of Ottawa (the market place is pictured above) had been the capital of Canada for ten years. Ottawa came into being in the late 1820s and was soon important in the timber trade. By 1868 it was a typical thriving colonial city showing that rough-and-ready realism which characterized most settlements in rich, rapidly developing lands. The contrast with Victorian England is typified in the picture below of a Victorian gentleman in his carriage. The upper strata of England's society exhibited a respectable and cultured opulence which is well illustrated in this picture.

1868 BENJAMIN DISRAELI (1804-81). Son of a Jewish man of letters, he was perhaps the most original and interesting of Victorian statesmen. Baptized a Christian at the age of thirteen, he was thereby enabled to enter the House of Commons as a Tory in 1837; professing Jews were not admitted until 1858. Even before his election he was famous as a novelist, pamphleteer, wit and dandy. The prophet of Tory democracy, he believed that "gentry" and people were natural allies. He was leader of the Conservative party from 1850 onwards, and Premier in 1868 and again in 1874. He was responsible for the second great electoral reform bill, and for Britain's obtaining a controlling interest in the Suez Canal. Disraeli was created Earl of Beaconsfield in 1876.

1868 GLADSTONE'S FIRST MINISTRY. The Gladstone government of 1868-74 established the national elementary education system and introduced the ballot. Below, Gladstone is seen reading at the near corner of the table; John Bright stands behind him, and Lord Hartington, afterwards succeeding as Duke of Devonshire, is on the extreme right.

1869 OPENING OF THE SUEZ CANAL. It is believed that there was a canal
between the Red Sea and the Nile Delta as early as 1380 B.C., but none
had been navigable since A.D. 800. The modern canal, whose engineer and promoter

was a Frenchman, Ferdinand de Lesseps, used some of those earlier, long derelict, stretches of waterway. It was opened in December, 1869, by a procession of ships of all nations, headed by the French "Aigle" with the Empress Eugénie on board.

75

1870 LORD TENNYSON (1809-92). He published his first volume in 1830 and his last in 1892, so that his production covers practically the whole of the Queen's reign. His popularity reached its zenith about 1870, but the parts of his work most admired nowadays were chiefly written before 1850, the year in which he was appointed to the laureateship in succession to Wordsworth. He remained a remarkably prolific writer whose versatility increased with his years, and in 1884, after much hesitation, he accepted a peerage. Of subsequent poets, only Kipling has approached Tennyson's wide popularity with the general public.

1870 HANS CHRISTIAN AN-DERSEN (1805-75). Son of a Danish cobbler, he became world famous as a writer of fairy tales, largely drawn from the folk-lore passed on to him by his grandmother. Slow in obtaining recognition, he rose to be the friend of the Danish Royal Family, and on his seventieth birthday was honoured by a national festival at which he received an album containing one of his tales in fifteen languages—no exaggerated symbol of the international celebrity he had then achieved. He died unmarried, but surrounded by friends, at Copenhagen.

1870 CHARLES DICKENS (1812-70). Unlike Andersen, Dickens attained literary celebrity at an early age. His "Pickwick Papers" appeared in 1836-7, and from then onwards his success was assured. He was essentially a "popular" author, with an enormous public. In 1846 he became the first editor of the "Daily News," but resigned a few weeks later. He established the magazine "Household Words" in 1850. Towards the end of his life he amassed large sums by giving public readings from his works. He is remembered for the large number of characters found in his works whose names are recognized household words.

1870 LEWIS CARROLL (1832-98). A distinguished mathematician and a poet, the Rev. Charles Lutwidge Dodgson achieved immortality with his books, published under the name Lewis Carroll, "Alice's Adventures in Wonderland" and "Through the Looking-Glass." Both books, which have retained an astonishing hold on succeeding generations of readers, have been translated into many languages, and "Alice" has been dramatized and filmed. The "Alice" MS. was sold in the U.S. for more than £30,000—a measure of the value which Americans set upon his peerless fantasies.

1870 VICTORIAN DRAMA. In the early 1850s the British theatre was at a very low ebb, and it is largely owing to Queen Victoria's influence that it gained so notably in prestige during the succeeding decades. By 1870 the London stage contained a number of commanding personalities, of whom the picture above shows a group from the play "Dearer than Life," including Charles Wyndham, standing, left; J. L. Toole, seated, left; and Henry Irving, seated, extreme right. Below, Madge Kendal and her husband, William Kendal, are seen in "Diplomacy" at the Prince of Wales' Theatre a few years later. These five names, famous even today among playgoers, give the measure of this age of great Victorian acting.

1870 FRANCO-PRUSSIAN WAR. From the outset things went badly for the French, who completely failed to match their opponents in organization and leadership. On 1 September Napoleon III and the principal French army were surrounded by the Prussians at Sedan and forced to capitulate the next day. Above, Bismarck is receiving the French surrender. This virtually decided the issue of the war. Paris was invested, but on 7 October Gambetta, a young lawyer, Minister of Defence in the newly formed Republican Government, escaped by balloon from the capital and inspired the brave but hopeless resistance which dragged on in the provinces for several months. The balloon is seen being inflated.

1871 WILLIAM PROCLAIMED GERMAN EMPEROR. On 18 January, 1871, William I of Prussia was proclaimed Emperor of Germany in the Hall of Mirrors, Versailles— later the scene of the peace treaty at which Germany was humiliated after the First World War. As shown in the picture above, the crown was formally offered to William by the King of Bavaria.

1871 STREET BARRIER AT PLACE VENDÔME, PARIS. The end of the Franco-Prussian War was immediately followed by a violent insurrection in Paris, known as the "Commune." The Place Vendôme was a masterpiece of French classical architecture, but for a brief space was the scene of a typical barricade, such as that seen here, during the disturbances.

1871 JOHN STUART MILL (1806-73). Here seen with his wife, he was an original and influential political thinker. His "Political Economy" was a standard treatise in economics. Entering Parliament, he moved a women's suffrage amendment to the 1867 Reform Bill. Perhaps precocity of thought came naturally to a man who started learning Greek at the remarkably early age of four!

1871 READY FOR THE ROAD. The lady below was a very ordinary sight at this time. Riding was still the able-bodied person's common means of travelling any distance on the roads. Our equestrienne is holding the "billycock" hat which was supposed to break a fall, and, of course, her mount is equipped with a side-saddle, which can be clearly seen in the picture.

1871 GREAT FIRE OF CHICAGO.
In 1804 the U.S. Government
established a military post called Fort
Dearborn. By 1871 this had become the
great city of Chicago. Mainly built of
wood, it fell a ready victim to the
devastating fire which broke out on
8 October. The fire, which is said to
have travelled two and a half miles
in six and a half hours, rendered a
hundred thousand people homeless,
and some idea of the destruction is
gained from the lower picture, which
is reproduced from a photograph
taken early in 1872. A relief fund
opened in Great Britain realized over
£100,000—a vast sum in those days.

1872 "CHALLENGER" EXPEDITION. The modest little ship seen here, in Bermuda dockyard, was in 1872 sent out by the British Government on one of the world's most famous expeditions to explore the ocean and the sea bed. Its operations lasted until 1876, and the reports of the scientists who took part extended to some fifty highly important volumes.

1873 GIRL STUDENT AT CAMBRIDGE. The illustration below, of a girl student in her study at a Cambridge college, carries us back to an important point in the development of women's education. Girton College for women was founded at Hitchin in 1869, and transferred to Cambridge itself in 1873. Oxford followed this example some years later.

1873 DEATH OF DR. LIVINGSTONE.
David Livingstone, Scottish missionary and explorer, who died in 1873, set off in 1865, without any white companion, on his third journey into the African interior. In 1869 it occurred to the editor of "The New York Herald" that the discovery of his whereabouts would make big news. H. M. Stanley, a Welsh workhouse boy who had become an American journalist, was sent to find Livingstone, which he did in 1871 on the shores of Lake Tanganyika. Stanley remained with his host for about four months and then returned. In no sense of the word did he "rescue" him, as has so often been claimed. Livingstone continued his search for the source of the Nile until his death. This illustration depicts the famous meeting between the Scot and the Welshman. The latter, here seen armed and with an escort, later earned more merited fame as an independent explorer.

1873 SANKEY AND MOODY MISSION IN LONDON. Ira D. Sankey and Dwight L. Moody were American evangelists from Chicago. From 1873 to 1875 they conducted in Great Britain a mission which drew enormous congregations and made an extraordinary impression on people of all classes. Moody was the preacher, of an intensely emotional type, while Sankey composed and sang popular hymns. It was a pity, he said, that the Devil should have all the best tunes! One of their most striking successes was at Cambridge, where some socially and athletically notable young men, "The Cambridge Seven," decided, under the inspiration of Sankey and Moody, to devote their lives to mission work. In this illustration Moody is seen in the pulpit of the Agricultural Hall, Islington, with Sankey behind him. The enormous congregation depicted in this contemporary print is entirely typical of the tremendous numbers who flocked to hear them.

85

1875 ALEXANDRA, PRINCESS OF WALES, AND FAMILY. The Prince of Wales and Princess Alexandra of Denmark were married in 1863. She was one of the most beautiful women of her day. Her London home, Marlborough House, became a centre of fashion such as Queen Victoria's court never aspired to be. Of her two sons seen in the picture opposite, the elder, Albert Victor, Duke of Clarence, died with tragic suddenness in 1892, and the younger, George, Duke of York, in 1910 became King George V. Also in the picture are the Princesses Louise and Maude (standing) and Princess Victoria, seated in the foreground.

1875 THE PRINCE'S FIRST TIGER. The visit of the Prince of Wales to India was an item of Disraeli's twofold policy to bring the Royal Family into the limelight and to make the British public Empire-conscious. The Prince left England on 11 October, 1875, and was received at Bombay by the Viceroy. Here he met many Indian Princes and afterwards visited them at their courts. In doing so he travelled 8,000 miles and, it was said at the time, saw more of India than any living Englishman. In the group below he is seen holding his gun after making a successful début in that traditional sport of the Englishman in India, tiger-hunting.

1876 "NEW CROWNS FOR OLD." Above is a famous "Punch" cartoon by Sir John Tenniel, illustrator of "Alice in Wonderland," to celebrate the assumption by Queen Victoria of the title Empress of India. Disraeli, in 1876, carried through Parliament a bill conferring this title on the Queen, the proclamation taking place early the following year. This title was relinquished by the British Crown in 1948, when India and Pakistan respectively achieved their present status.

1877 TEMPLE BAR ARCHWAY. Temple Bar, at the Strand end of Fleet Street, has been famous for centuries as one of the old London gates. This archway designed by Christopher Wren was put up in 1672 to take the place of an earlier gate. It remained until 1878, becoming an increasing impediment to Victorian traffic, though this Sunday morning photograph shows nothing of the chaos it caused. The arch was re-erected in Theobald's Park, Cheshunt, Hertfordshire.

1878 CONGRESS OF BERLIN. In 1877 Russia declared war on Turkey and compelled her to accept the Treaty of San Stefano, creating a "Bulgaria" (a mere puppet of Russia) extending to the Black Sea. Beaconsfield demanded a revision of the treaty on the ground that Turkish frontiers were a common interest of all Europe. At the subsequent Congress held in Berlin, Bismarck (seen centre, with white moustache) presided and the desired frontier revision was achieved. Beaconsfield, on his return, claimed that he had brought back "peace with honour." Three successive British Conservative Premiers were present: Beaconsfield (seen standing near the corner of the table), Lord Salisbury (then Foreign Secretary), and the young A. J. Balfour, who was at that time his Private Secretary.

1878 BRITISH WARSHIPS AT MALTA. The picture shows three of the old style and one of the new. This last is "Thunderer" (1873), which "provided the general pattern followed in fighting ships" up to the "Dreadnought" of 1905. Shown bottom left in this picture, she was the first warship with a modern silhouette, with two turrets and a single stumpy iron mast, which was placed, with her two funnels and top hamper, amidships between the turrets. She and her sister ship, "Devastation," were 285 ft. long, having a displacement of 9,320 tons and a speed of 14 knots. There was no provision for sail. The other ships are, of course, survivals of the age of combined steam and sail—more picturesque but less efficient.

1878 VICTORIAN HOUSE-HOLD. This picture is just an item from the family album, but eloquent of the leisurely times enjoyed by middle-class families of that date. It was entirely in character that the gardener should be invited into the complete family group—although, it need hardly be said, he "knew his place!"

1878 TENNIS AT HOMBURG. Lawn tennis, so recently developed in England, was introduced by Sir Robert Anstruther to Homburg, the celebrated German health resort. Below we see Sir Robert, right, on far side of net, and other pioneers partaking in a rather primitive-looking demonstration. Note the 5-ft. net specified in the M.C.C. rules of 1875. Had this been continued the modern "cannon-ball" service would obviously have been impossible.

1879 ZULU WAR: RORKE'S DRIFT. The Zulu War of 1878-9 was undertaken
without Government sanction by the British High Commissioner, Sir Bartle
Frere, who thought that the Zulus were a menace to the Transvaal and Natal.
The war opened with the slaughter of a British force at Isandhlwana, but Britain's
reputation was retrieved at Rorke's Drift, where 103 men defended their position
against some thousands of Zulus and drove them off with heavy loss. Lieutenants
Chard and Bromhead, whom this contemporary picture shows in animated discussion,
won the V.C. for their leadership in this exploit. Six months later the Zulu chief
Cetywayo was routed and his military strength annihilated at Ulundi.

93

1879 SECOND AFGHAN WAR. This campaign resulted from an attempt to establish British control of the government of Afghanistan. The British leader in the field was Sir Frederick (later Lord) Roberts, V.C., here seen inspecting captured Afghan artillery. "Bobs" was one of the best-loved soldiers in British military history. He won the V.C. as a young man during the Indian Mutiny and

established his reputation as a brilliant commander during the Afghan War of 1879-80, which is generally regarded as the highest achievement of the British and Indian armies during the Victorian era. Twenty years later, Roberts was appointed Commander-in-Chief in South Africa after "Black Week." The Afghan policy followed by the Beaconsfield Government was later abandoned by Gladstone.

1879 TAY BRIDGE DISASTER. The railway viaduct across the Firth of Tay, nearly two miles long, was opened in 1877. During the night of 28 December, 1879, in a gale, the central portion collapsed while a train was crossing. All ninety passengers were killed. This picture was taken on the following day.

1880 COUNTRY HOUSE PARTY. The group below, with its air of peace and confidence, exhibits a feature worthy of notice. The wicker garden chairs endured until the end of the Queen's reign. Uncomfortable to sit in and unwieldy to carry, they were finally ousted by the convenient folding "deck" chair.

1880 CRICKET GIANTS. Dr. W. G. Grace (1848-1918), seen right, came of a cricketing family and started playing almost as soon as he could walk. He appeared for the Gentlemen against the Players every year from 1865 to 1900, and in Test matches from their inception till 1899. Figures tell only part of his story; apart from his record as a batsman and bowler he changed the whole outlook of cricketers and the cricketing public, for his personality was as remarkable as his skill. The first representative Australian team to tour England caused a sensation in 1878 by beating a powerful home eleven in a single day. Their 1880 successors were honoured with a full "Test" match, in which Grace scored 152 for England and Murdoch 153 not out for Australia. England won by 5 wickets. Below, the players are: Back row: G. E. Palmer, W. H. Moule, G. J. Bonnor, G. Alexander, T. U. Groube. Middle row: F. R. Spofforth, H. F. Boyle, W. L. Murdoch, P. S. M'Donnell, A. C. Bannerman. Front row: A. H. Jarvis, J. Slight, J. M. Blackham.

1882 BOMBARDMENT OF ALEXANDRIA. The events leading up to the British bombardment of Alexandria on 11 July, 1882, are extremely complicated. In 1876 the Khedive (Sultan) of Egypt suspended payment of his debts, mostly interest on loans from British and French bondholders, whereupon the British and French Governments established a dual control of Egyptian finance to "advise" the Khedive's ministers in matters of economy. The Egyptian Army, disliking the irregularity of its pay, rebelled in 1881 and overthrew the Khedive's Government. Britain and France now had "to get on or get out." France got out; Britain got on. The bombardment of Alexandria by the British Fleet was the first, and Sir Garnet Wolseley's desert victory of Tel-el-Kebir was the last, act of a brief war which gave Britain control of Egypt. This picture shows the British Fleet lying off the Harbour after the bombardment and some of the damage it did to an Egyptian fort. Lord Cromer took charge for twenty-four years and gave Egypt "justice and water"—that is, scientific irrigation. British "rule" lasted until 1922, and was, on the whole, of real benefit to Egypt, though that country was never legally within the Empire. The chief British official was styled "Agent and Consul-General." Even after the Treaty of 1922 Britain retained the right to maintain forces in Egypt, a right of immense significance on the outbreak of the Second World War.

1882 BILLINGSGATE MARKET. This picture shows the celebrated London fishmarket on the Thames, immediately above the Custom House, as it was in 1882. It was established as a Free Market in 1699, having long been a convenient anchorage for small vessels. However, it is a mere youngster among London markets, that at Leadenhall being known to have existed in 1411 and Smithfield in the reign of Henry II (1154-89). From early Saxon times, and for centuries afterwards, the Port of London included the two "hithes," or landing places, of Queenhithe and Billingsgate. The increasing size of ships, coupled with the impediment offered by London Bridge, gradually led to the former's obsolescence. Billingsgate, in turn, proved unable to handle the full volume of traffic, and many other "legal quays" were established, leaving Billingsgate to specialize in the fish trade. The connexion between fish and bad language is obscure, but is not confined to England. "Billingsgate" is an old word for bad language, and the French "harangue," which we have anglicized and made respectable, is said to have been originally derived from the language used by those who dealt in herrings.

1883 LONDON TELEPHONE EXCHANGE.
The telephone, like education and so many other things, was started by private enterprise and was only "socialized" later on. Graham Bell and Thomas Alva Edison independently invented telephone apparatus, and secured British patents in 1876-7. The resulting companies amalgamated in 1880 and commenced operations. This picture shows that women played a vital part from the very first in this new form of communication. Even two years after the date of the picture there were but 3,800 telephone users in London and less than 10,000 in the rest of the country. The telephone was taken over by the Post Office in 1912, by which date its use had become much more widely established.

1886 CANADIAN PACIFIC RAILWAY. In 1867 the Atlantic and Pacific Oceans were first linked by rail across the United States. In the same year the British North American colonies were federated in a single Dominion of Canada, and British Columbia made her adhesion conditional on her being given railway connexion with the East across the almost unoccupied prairie belt. This railway project was a vast undertaking for a country of barely four million people, but it was completed in 1886, the last spike being driven in by Donald Smith (Lord Strathcona), a millionaire who had backed the scheme with all his resources. These illustrations show, respectively, the very necessary armed guard on part of the prairie line during construction; the first regular trans-Continental train (at Fernie, B.C.); and, below, a stage coach typical of those which for many years continued to "feed" the railway on the less populous branch routes.

103

1885 DEATH OF GENERAL GORDON. When Britain took control of Egypt she was faced with the problem of the Sudan, conquered by Egypt fifty years earlier and now in the hands of "dervishes," religious fanatics led by the "Mahdi." Gladstone's Government sent Gordon out to investigate. He was besieged in Khartoum, where he was murdered when the dervishes captured it. The relieving British force arrived two days too late, on 28 January, 1885.

1885 THE FIRST MOTOR-CAR. Gottlieb Daimler, a German, patented the internal-combustion engine in 1885, and had his first motor-car, seen here, on the roads during the same year. Motoring made rapid strides in Germany and France, but was hampered in Britain by the "Red Flag Act" (see page 43) until 1896. During that period Britain's only contribution to motoring was the pneumatic tyre, invented by Dunlop in 1887.

1885 BEGINNINGS OF JOHANNESBURG. In 1881, after Majuba, the Dutch farmers of the Transvaal recovered their independence. In 1885 what proved the richest goldfield in the world was discovered on the ridge of hills called the Rand. Foreigners (Uitlanders), mostly British, flocked in and Johannesburg was born, to become the largest city in South Africa. This view of its beginnings provides an astonishing contrast with the city of today. In the foreground are the workings of an early gold-mine.

1886 FRANZ LISZT (1811-86). Hungarian by birth, Liszt was one of the great personalities of nineteenth-century music. As a pianist his brilliance had a lasting influence on technique. He left many original pianoforte compositions, as well as famous transcriptions of Beethoven's symphonies. A man of powerful personality and immense learning, he wrote eloquently on music and musicians, was a potent champion of Berlioz and Wagner and received a patent of nobility from the Austrian Emperor. This photograph was taken shortly before his death.

1887 QUEEN VICTORIA'S JUBILEE. On completing the fiftieth year of her reign, the Queen was sixty-eight and already had great-grandchildren, sons of the future Kaiser. Her reign had marked, for the people as a whole, a period of almost unbroken peace, growing prosperity and social reforms. Her interventions in matters of government are said sometimes to have embarrassed her ministers, but they, like the nation at large, had a strong and lasting affection for their monarch.

The Queen is photographed here in her ceremonial robes.

1887 HENLEY REGATTA. The first English regatta, a form of sport copied from
Venice and retaining its Italian name, was held on the Thames at Ranelagh
in 1775. Thenceforward the Thames became a centre for such events, and Henley-
on-Thames, thirty miles west of London, with its long, straight reach, is ideally

situated for them. Henley Regatta was established as an annual midsummer festival in 1839 and the race for the Diamond Sculls was inaugurated five years later. The picture shows the finish of "the Diamonds" in 1887. Oxford and Cambridge had held their first contest with eights in 1829, transferring to Putney-Mortlake in 1845.

1890 TROOPSHIP FOR THE FAR EAST.
Queen Victoria's loyal subjects were fond of recalling that Britain had not seen a gun fired in anger during the whole of her reign. Nevertheless, numerous small wars kept units of the army busy in many parts of the world, while the nation's overseas commitments and responsibilities were increasing in other areas where no actual fighting took place. In consequence, a growing number of British troops saw service thousands of miles from their home country. The lot of the soldier on a troopship has never been enviable. In the days of sail it was wellnigh intolerable for months on end. With the establishment of steam as the recognized motive power conditions improved and the journeys became quicker. The troops on the "Euphrates," shown in this picture leaving Portsmouth for Aden and the Far East, were near enough to a far worse era to congratulate themselves on their relatively good luck.

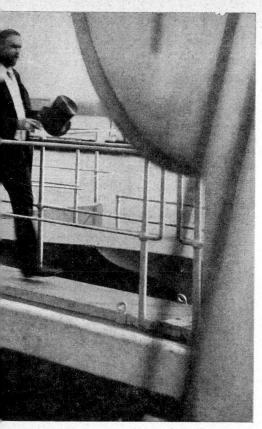

1889 VISIT OF THE GERMAN EMPEROR TO BRITAIN. This was one of the frequent visits to Britain made by Kaiser Wilhelm II, who had succeeded his father the previous year. The Kaiser liked to remember his relationship with the British Royal Family, but also he could never forget that he was Emperor of a State which was coming into more and more conscious rivalry with Great Britain. A grandson of Queen Victoria, he came to the throne at the age of 29, and at once commenced to assert his independence of Bismarck, who had so successfully guided his country's destinies for a quarter of a century. The two men came into irreconcilable opposition, and a year after the date of the visit shown here Wilhelm startled the world by "dropping the pilot." In this picture he is second in the procession; behind him come the Prince of Wales (later Edward VII), Prince Henry of Prussia and Prince Albert Victor (Duke of Clarence and elder brother of the future George V), who died tragically in 1892.

1893 THE LOSS OF H.M.S. "VICTORIA."
One of the great naval tragedies of the Victorian era occurred off Tripoli, Syria, on 22 June, 1893, when the "Victoria," during manoeuvres, was rammed and sunk by H.M.S. "Camperdown," with a loss of 358 officers and men. "Victoria" and "Camperdown" were leading two parallel columns and the disaster arose through the admiral, Sir George Tryon, in "Victoria," trying to turn the columns inwards with insufficient space. Tryon went down with his ship. The vessel, here seen disappearing in a cloud of steam and spray, had been launched six years earlier. On a displacement of 10,470 tons she carried two 16·25-in., one 10-in. and smaller guns.

1893 "GENTLEMEN v. PLAYERS" AT LORD'S. This reproduction of a painting by Dickinson and Foster shows a typical gathering in the pavilion on a big day at the headquarters of cricket. W. G. Grace is unmistakable in the centre of the stage; and among the many famous players on view are John Shuter, talking to "W.G."; C. J. Kortright, in the bottom right-hand corner, and reputedly the fastest bowler in the world; and A. G. Steel, behind Shuter. A. C. Maclaren stands facing Kortright. Notice, too, the important little group of professionals on the Players' Balcony. The figure at the near end is that of Surrey's fast bowler of many seasons, Tom Richardson. At the far end, close to the stationary coach, is the one and only George Hirst, perhaps most characteristic of all Yorkshire's great cricketers. But there is a dazzling galaxy of peers, parliamentarians and assorted celebrities—to such a pitch of popularity had Grace's prestige brought Britain's summer game among all classes in the land.

113

1893 WEDDING OF THE DUKE AND DUCHESS OF YORK, afterwards King George V and Queen Mary. The bride, known as Princess May before her marriage, was herself a great-granddaughter of King George III through one of his younger sons, the Duke of Cambridge. The bridal pair were thus second cousins once removed. In the group shown above the bride and bridegroom are easily distinguishable. On the left as one looks at the picture are (standing, left to right): Princess Alexandra of Edinburgh, aged 15 at the time; Princess Victoria of Schleswig-Holstein, aged 23; and Princess Victoria of Edinburgh, 17. In the second row are the 8-year-old Princess Alice of Battenberg and Princess Margaret of Connaught, aged 11; while seated at their feet is Princess Beatrice of Edinburgh, who was 9. Standing to the left of the Duke of York are his sisters, Princess Victoria of Wales, 25, and Princess Maud of Wales, who was two years younger. The two children seated at the bottom right-hand corner of the picture are 6-year-old Princess Victoria of Battenberg and, one year her senior, Princess Victoria Patricia, daughter of the Duke of Connaught. The last-named princess, better known as "Princess Pat," contracted a romantic marriage in 1919 to a young naval officer, the Hon. A. R. M. Ramsay, later a distinguished British admiral.

1894 CECIL RHODES AND KIMBERLEY NOTABLES. Seen above in the centre of the front row, Rhodes was now forty-one years old. He was sent out to South Africa for his health at the age of seventeen, showed himself a brilliant financier and made a fortune. His later efforts were devoted to building an all-British Africa. He was Prime Minister of Cape Colony, 1890-6.

1894 OPENING OF THE MANCHESTER SHIP CANAL. Begun in 1887, this canal enables ocean-going ships to travel thirty-four miles from the Mersey estuary to Manchester. It brought quick profits to Manchester as a whole, but many years elapsed before it could pay dividends to shareholders. This photograph shows the Chairman's yacht making the first trip on the canal.

1894 TRIAL OF ALFRED DREYFUS. The Dreyfus case constituted a prolonged scandal in French politics. A Jewish captain in the French Army, Dreyfus was accused in 1894 of authorship of a schedule of secret documents which were to be sold to Germany. He was court-martialled and sentenced to life imprisonment. A year later Colonel Picquart, of the French War Ministry, pressed unsuccessfully for the case to be reopened. Then Émile Zola, the novelist, took up the cudgels on Dreyfus's behalf in his famous open letter, "J'accuse." In 1899 the case was retried at Rennes, where in the lower picture Dreyfus is shown facing his judges. He was again found guilty, but with "extenuating circumstances," and "pardoned," although already the real culprit was known. Six years later his innocence was officially acknowledged and he was reinstated in the French Army.

1896 JAMESON'S RAID. Foreigners engaged in gold mining around Johannesburg were subjected to many petty tyrannies by Kruger's Transvaal Government. Cecil Rhodes, Prime Minister of Cape Colony, hoped to use the discontent of these Uitlanders to overthrow Kruger. There was to be a rising of Uitlanders, which Starr Jameson would support by invading the Transvaal with 470 Bechuanaland Mounted Police. But the Uitlanders did not rise. Jameson invaded without orders, his party being surrounded by superior Boer forces and forced to surrender four days later at Doornkop, as shown above. In the lower picture Jameson, second from left, standing, and his officers are seen on board ship returning to England for trial. He was sentenced to fifteen months' imprisonment, but released after six months.

117

1896 KLONDIKE GOLD RUSH. From 1896 until the end of the century, when the supply began to peter out, gold was discovered in several valleys of the Klondike region in N.W. Canada. Dawson City, the chief settlement, founded on a permanently frozen peat bog, attained for a time a population of 10,000. Thanks to the Canadian Mounted Police, this gold rush was singularly free from crimes of violence, and certainly the typical prospectors shown in this picture look peaceful enough.

1896 REVIVAL OF THE OLYMPIC GAMES.

The ancient Olympic Games, held every fourth year at Olympia in the Peloponnese, were a great unifying institution for the free cities of classical Greece. The first recorded celebration was in 776 B.C.; the 293rd, and last, in A.D. 393. The earliest contests seem to have been tests of endurance to which, in time, were added chariot races, horse and foot races, jumping, throwing quoits and the javelin, and a mixture of wrestling and boxing. The revival in 1896 at Athens was encouraged by the Greek Government and the Games were opened to all nations. This photograph of the Games in progress shows the crowds thronging the specially built stadium. Subsequently, the "modern Olympics" have been held at various European capitals and once at Los Angeles, in California. The programme nowadays is long and varied, but with the accent strongly on "track" and "field" athletic events.

1897 QUEEN VICTORIA'S DIAMOND JUBILEE. On 21 June, 1897, was celebrated not only the longest reign of the most venerated sovereign in British history, but the climax of an unprecedented imperial prosperity. The central event was a service on the steps of St. Paul's Cathedral, and the procession seen here.

1896 OTTO LILIENTHAL GLIDING. The art of gliding by the skilful use of air currents prepared the way for flight in heavier-than-air machines propelled by engines. Possibly the most distinguished of all the pioneer gliders was the German, Otto Lilienthal, here seen during one of the two thousand successful flights which he made before he was killed in 1896 at the age of forty-eight. He demonstrated the advantages of cambered wings for flight, and so led the way directly to the design of the machine which enabled the Wrights to achieve powered flight seven years later, they being keen students of his recorded observations.

1898 SINKING OF THE "MAINE." For years the Cubans, strongly supported by the American public, had been in rebellion against the Spanish colonial government. On 15 February, 1898, the U.S. cruiser "Maine" was sunk by explosion in Havana harbour. The cause of the explosion remains a mystery, and it is most unlikely that Spain would have committed so suicidal an act of provocation. America, however, seized on the pretext for war, and with vastly superior forces overwhelmed the Spaniards in a brief campaign. The illustrations show two views of the wreckage during the lengthy period when it was being examined by experts.

1898 KITCHENER'S SUDAN CAMPAIGN. Sir Herbert Kitchener, born in 1850, first achieved world fame in 1898 when, as "Sirdar" and Commander-in-Chief of the Anglo-Egyptian Army, he penetrated the Nile valley with a force which constructed its own railways as it went along, reconquered the Sudan and destroyed the forces of the Khalifa, successor to that Mahdi who had slain Gordon thirteen years before. The decisive battle was fought at Omdurman, close to Khartoum. The entire campaign was the first famous example of that complete attention to detail upon which Kitchener's tremendous reputation was largely founded. The photograph reproduced here shows the British general as he was first known to millions of his admiring fellow - countrymen, while below is the Mahdi's Tomb. The damage visible was caused by the British bombardment just after the Battle of Omdurman.

1898 MARCHAND AND THE FASHODA INCIDENT.

Relations between Britain and France were far from friendly in the last years of the century. In 1896 the British and Egyptian Governments announced their intention to reconquer the Sudan from the dervishes, and issued a warning that any French intervention on the Upper Nile would be regarded as "an unfriendly act." In spite of this, a small French expedition under Major Marchand, seen right, was sent eastward from French Equatorial Africa, and just as Kitchener was occupying Khartoum, Marchand hoisted the French flag at Fashoda, 600 miles farther up the Nile. The British at once demanded a withdrawal, but not until February, 1899, did the French abandon their claims. The picture shows members of the expedition, including coloured infantry, after their return to France, being wildly cheered by a rabidly anti-British Paris mob.

1898 PIERRE AND MARIE CURIE DISCOVER RADIUM. Pierre Curie, a professor at Paris University, and his wife, a Pole, were jointly responsible for the discovery of this boon to mankind. Curie was killed in a street accident in 1906 and his wife continued researches alone. They are seen here in their laboratory.

1899 FOUR GENERATIONS OF ROYALTY. Here we have Queen Victoria (born 1819), the Prince of Wales (1841), the Duke of York (1865) and little Prince Edward (1894), between them destined to occupy Britain's throne for only six months short of one hundred years. At her death two years later the Queen had the impressive total of thirty-seven great-grandchildren.

1899 TWO AMERICAN PRESIDENTS. When the picture below was taken William McKinley, left, was President of the U.S. and his companion, Theodore Roosevelt, the next Vice-President. In 1901 McKinley was assassinated, to be succeeded by Roosevelt, a far greater man than he. The new President was re-elected in 1904 and before he went out of office in 1909 had proved himself to be a statesman of world stature and one who fully deserved the Nobel Peace Prize awarded him in 1906.

1899 AT THE HEART OF LONDON. This picture, identical in background with that on pages 34-35, shows the cumulative effect of fifty years' steady change. The vehicles are still horse-drawn, but have been entirely redesigned and are severely "functional." The road surface has been modernized to deal with the

far greater volume of traffic which has developed. Fashions have taken a turn which clearly foreshadows those of the twentieth century. The custom of advertising commercial wares on every type of commercial vehicle is now clearly established. The City's centre now looks what it is—the hub of a great metropolis.

1900 BOXER REBELLION. This rebellion was organized by a group of Chinese whose forces besieged the European legations in Peking for several weeks. Above are shown Chinese troops who, although sent against the Boxers, fraternized with them. The legations were ultimately relieved by European forces.

1900 KAISER WILHELM II AND HIS TROOPS. The Kaiser was fond of "playing with soldiers," as in the illustration below, and the German Army was the most efficient in the world. Britain became far more concerned when, about this time, Wilhelm started to build a fleet to challenge British naval superiority.

1900 PLEASURES OF VICTORIAN TIMES. The origins of the Hampstead Heath fair can be traced back almost to time immemorial. This view of the fairground in 1900 with Parliament Hill Fields in the background shows that, except for the clothes of the visitors, it had even then established a character, with its helterskelter, swings and coconut shies, which has endured with very few changes to our own day. Cycling, as symbolized by the contemporary picture from Hyde Park, was more novel. In 1885 J. K. Starley invented the "safety" (i.e. chain-driven) bicycle, and in 1887 Dunlop followed with the pneumatic tyre. On this dual basis were laid the foundations of the cycling craze which reached its peak in the mid-'nineties and ensuing years. Cycling, for a while, was not merely a means of transport, but, as shown here, a fashionable pastime which large crowds gathered to witness.

1900 TWO BOER LEADERS. These two were the man of the past and the man of the future in Dutch South Africa at the time. Paul Kruger (1825-1904), left, became President of the Transvaal Republic in 1883, after Majuba. Shrewd but stubborn, he was strongly anti-British in outlook, and disappeared from history when he fled before the advancing British armies in 1900. In the same year Louis Botha (1862-1919), below, became Commander-in-Chief of the Transvaal Boer armies. He opposed the war with Britain but, once it had commenced, proved a formidable opponent. With the death of Joubert, Botha became Commander-in-Chief of the Boer forces, and when all was hopeless he persuaded his countrymen to accept the British peace terms at Vereeniging. After the war he accepted the idea of a united, self-governing South Africa within the British Empire and worked wholeheartedly for its achievement. In 1910 he became the first Premier of the Union of South Africa, holding office until he died.

1900 MARCHING TO JOHANNESBURG. The South African War began in October, 1899, and went badly for Britain because the Boers were prepared and the British were not. Boer columns, invading British territory, invested Ladysmith, Kimberley and Mafeking. The two former were relieved in February, 1900. Roberts and Kitchener, based on Cape Town, commenced the movement which occupied Johannesburg on 31 May. Above are seen the 84th Battery and Balloon Corps during this march. Balloons were no innovation, as they had been used spasmodically for observation purposes since the French Revolutionary wars.

1900 LONG TOM AT MAFEKING. The Creuzot gun shown, right, being fired by the Boers at Mafeking was one of those which Kruger imported from France with a view to driving the British out of South Africa. The siege, though not in itself very important, attracted world-wide attention, partly by reason of its long duration, partly from the gaiety of the messages which Col. Baden-Powell, who commanded the garrison, contrived to get through to the outside world. When at last Mafeking was relieved after 217 days, rejoicing in Britain was such as to introduce a new word, "mafficking," into the English language, to signify immoderate celebration of some event by large crowds.

134

1900 BATTLE OF PAARDEBERG. The biggest, and decisive, pitched battle of the South African War was fought at Paardeberg between the redoubtable Cronje and his Boers and the British under Lords Roberts and Kitchener. Cronje repelled four attacks with heavy loss, but was finally surrounded and compelled to surrender with 4,000 men in February, 1900. He was sent a prisoner of war to St. Helena, while Roberts pressed on to Bloemfontein. Here, having regrouped his forces, he pushed ahead rapidly for Pretoria, which he entered on 5 June. Roberts, then a veteran of sixty-eight, is seen, left, with his staff supervising the moving up of British transport at Paardeberg. Roberts was created an earl, and from 1901 to 1904 was Commander-in-Chief of the British Army. He died in 1914 while visiting British troops in France during the First World War.

1901 AUSTRALIAN COMMONWEALTH PROCLAIMED. The first British settlement in Australia dates from 1788, and the five colonies of the mainland were granted self-government about the middle of the nineteenth century. Federation into a single Commonwealth was achieved in 1901, and, above, Lord Hopetoun is seen being sworn in as first Governor-General, in a special pavilion at Sydney.

1901 FLOWER-SELLERS AT PICCADILLY CIRCUS. The steps of the Shaftesbury Memorial Fountain, with Alfred Gilbert's beautiful sculpture of Eros, have long been a traditional site for flower-sellers such as those shown in this photograph.

1901 ISLINGTON FIRE BRIGADE. The picture below shows the very smart horse equipment typical of the London borough fire brigades at this date. Soon the petrol engine was to oust the more picturesque horse in this as in other spheres.

1901 FIRST TRANSATLANTIC WIRELESS SIGNAL. The top picture shows Marconi at Signal Hill, Newfoundland, with the instruments with which he received the first transatlantic wireless signals on 12 December, 1901. Below, some of his assistants are seen with the kite which carried the aerial to receive these messages, transmitted from Poldhu in Cornwall. Marconi, son of an Italian father and an Irish mother, was only twenty-seven at the time. He did not discover the principles of wireless telegraphy, but it was he who made it a commercial proposition, thus leading to its use for communications and, later, broadcasting.

1902 AIRSHIP AND AEROPLANE.
The problem of human flight has fascinated mankind for thousands of years. The first man to ascend in a gas-filled balloon was Rogier, in 1783. The invention of Daimler's internal-combustion engine in 1885 made powered flight immediately practicable and, in fact, the first of Zeppelin's airships appeared in 1900. On the right is seen Spencer's non-rigid airship crossing London in 1902. But the airship's supremacy was nearing an end. Little more than a year later—in December, 1903—the Wrights made the first authenticated flight, as shown below, at Kitty Hawk, North Carolina, in a power-driven heavier-than-air machine. A new era had arrived. Less than six years later Blériot had flown the English Channel (see page 19), and ten years later still Alcock and Brown flew non-stop across the Atlantic (see page 211).

1903 EDWARDIAN HOLIDAY. The scene here is distinctly different from that depicted on page 96. The male costume at least is nearer to that of our own day. The bowler-hatted gentleman in the background was one of the many thousands who, by accident or design, so ordered their facial decorations as to resemble as closely as possible the then Prince of Wales, afterwards King George V. The wide-brimmed hats of the two sons may strike a modern observer as more sensible summer wear than their stiff white collars, which were not to be discarded for many an uncomfortable year to come. As a group these people are certainly less stiff than those on page 96. The mother of the two boys (the facial resemblance is unmistakable) is even wearing the ghost of a smile! The wicker chairs have given place to permanent wooden garden seats such as can be seen on many a British railway station to this day. Far more significant, however, is the indication that children and young people are beginning to take that spontaneous interest in games which led to the inauguration of the Age of Sport between the First and Second World Wars. The rackets seem scarcely up to the best modern standards, but they reflect the wide popularity of the game of lawn tennis, then some twenty-five years old.

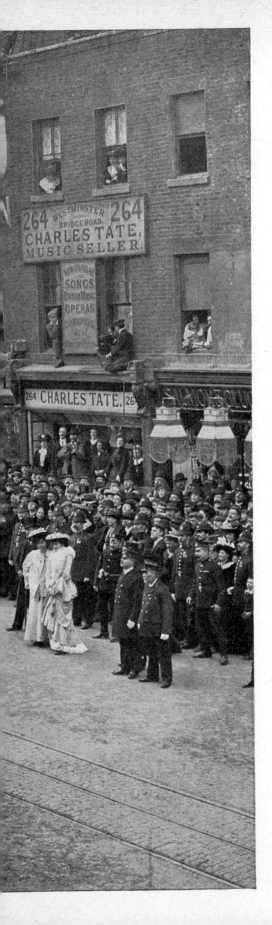

1903 THE L.C.C.'S FIRST ELECTRIC TRAM. As a general policy pursued for many years, successive London County Councils resisted the extension of trams, first horse-drawn and afterwards electric, into the central streets of the Metropolis. In this they were undoubtedly wise, since trams in busy streets are a major cause of traffic congestion. But the tram has exceptional passenger accommodation, and when, with the turn of the century, the well-designed electric tram made its appearance it obviously had a function to fulfil in Greater London. This illustration shows the inauguration of the first L.C.C. electric tram service in London in Westminster Bridge Road, quite close to the present County Hall. The ceremony was performed by the Prince of Wales (afterwards King George V), who is the farthest of the three figures seen on the driver's platform. Standing near-by is the Princess, afterwards Queen Mary. Within a relatively few years electric tramways had extended over hundreds of miles of streets, not only in London but also in most large provincial cities. For some reason not easy to understand, it was a good many years before the unfortunate top-deck passengers were given a roof over their heads. Scarcely had this overdue reform become general when the superior manoeuvring power of the trackless trolley-bus made it clear that the days of the tramway car were numbered. Finally, in 1950, a three-year plan was adopted for the complete elimination of the huge system of tracked trams in Greater London. Since London's first electric tram of all had been run by London United Tramways in 1901, the system had lasted for almost exactly half a century.

1904 SHADOWS OF WAR. The deterioration in relations between the European Great Powers led Britain and France to negotiate the "Entente Cordiale" of 1904. This was not an alliance but a settlement of colonial disputes between them in all parts of the world. To assist these new relations King Edward had visited Paris, to be greeted on the first day with cries of "Vivent les Boers!" but on the last with "Vive notre roi!" He is seen (marked with an X), top left, with President Loubet in Paris. Top right is one of the three damaged British fishing boats (one other was sunk) fired on by the Russian fleet in the North Sea during the same year in the course of the Russo-Japanese War. The incident was closed by payment of compensation. The bottom picture is that of the first British submarine, ordered by the Admiralty four years earlier, and here seen at Cowes. Not only by alliance but by a vast naval armaments programme did Britain prepare for the threatened danger.

145

1904-5 RUSSO-JAPANESE WAR. The Russian fleet which fired on British fishing boats (page 145) was on its way to Far Eastern waters, where it was duly destroyed by the Japanese in a series of actions which demonstrated Japan's efficiency as a naval power. There was also a vigorous war on land. Here, again, in spite of the gallantry of Russian troops seen in the two pictures above, Japan was victorious. The war itself marked a step in the struggle between Japan and Russia for control of North China and Korea. The Japanese victory hastened both the coming of the Russian revolution and the revolt of Asiatic peoples against European control. Its termination was largely due to the intervention of the American President, Theodore Roosevelt, through whom the terms of peace were agreed at the Treaty of Portsmouth, New Hampshire. On the right the peace conference is seen in session.

146

1905   A BUN FOR JUMBO. This picture of a huge elephant at the London Zoo, with a load of children on his back, accepting a bun from a well-dressed gentleman, reminds us how popular the Zoo had become even at that time. It was the first of its kind, opened in 1827 as a result of the efforts of Sir Stamford Raffles, who had already secured permanent world fame as the founder of Singapore.

1905 DEATH OF DR. BARNARDO. On 19 September died Dr. Thomas John Barnardo. Among the greatest of the Victorian philanthropists, he is seen above at one of the "Homes" which he founded. He opened his first one in 1867 at Stepney Causeway, London. Today over 100,000 children have entered them.

1905 ASCOT FASHIONS. Ascot is pre-eminently the royal and, as the lower illustration shows, even in 1905, the fashionable race meeting. The race-course was laid out by order of Queen Anne in 1711 and the famous royal procession, now an essential feature of the meeting, was instituted by George IV in 1820.

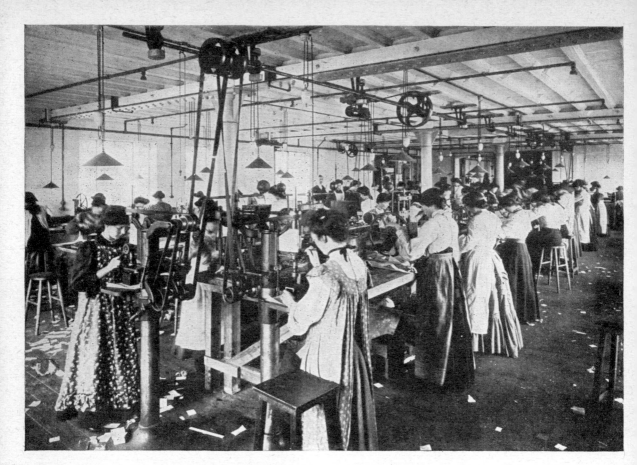

1906 WOMEN AT WORK AND PLAY. Above are seen women working in the Hall Street factory of the Wireless Telegraph and Signal Company, later the Marconi Wireless Telegraph Company. The illustration stresses not only the place of women in industry at this date, but the amount of wireless equipment which was already being turned out. In particular, wireless was being used to establish contact with ships at sea. Moreover, even in the decorous Edwardian days women were finding fresh fields to conquer. This picture of an early Furnival girls' rowing eight, although it shows the ladies more completely garbed than their present-day successors, aroused scandalized protests from many quarters. Oarsmen will note with respect that whereas the University eights are content with a blade apiece, these amazons manipulated two oars each, and seem to have had the audacity to keep pretty good time into the bargain.

1906 JOSEPH CHAMBERLAIN (1836-1914) captured the public attention as did no other statesman between the retirement of Gladstone (1894) and Lloyd George's "People's Budget" (1909). He entered the Commons as a Liberal in 1876, having not only made a fortune in Birmingham but also revolutionized its municipal government. Opposing Gladstone's Irish Home Rule Policy, he joined the Conservatives and became the leader of the imperialist movement. In 1903 he began his great campaign for the abandonment of Free Trade. A paralytic stroke ended his political career in 1906, and he died eight years later.

1906 H.M.S. "DREADNOUGHT" LAUNCHED. The famous battleship seen here was the creation of Sir John Fisher, perhaps the greatest naval administrator in British history. Its appearance with ten 12-in. guns at once reduced every other battleship afloat to the "second class." Henceforth the Anglo-German naval race was measured in terms of the number of "dreadnoughts" which each possessed. The Kiel Canal had to be widened to permit the passage of this class of ship and the widening was completed in 1914.

1906 KING ALFONSO'S WEDDING DAY. Alfonso XIII of Spain was born a King
on 17 May, 1886. Twenty years later, having been declared of age, he
married the niece of Britain's King Edward VII. It was Alfonso's misfortune to live in
troublesome times. Several attempts were made to murder the king and queen. The
remarkable photograph here reproduced shows the wedding-day bomb hurled at
the bridal coach by an alleged anarchist. Twenty-eight persons were killed, but
Alfonso and Ena behaved with the utmost coolness. Thereafter he made a number
of concessions to the rising tide of discontent, but the throne (rather than Alfonso
himself) was unpopular with an increasing number of people. The municipal elec-
tions of April, 1931, showed unmistakably the extent and intensity of the anti-
monarchist feeling. Alfonso and his family withdrew to exile in France, and the
votes of the people had done what the assassin's bomb failed to accomplish.

152

1907 EARLY MOTORING. The internal-combustion-engined motor-car in Britain was making up for lost time. The top picture shows a rally of Rolls-Royces at Buxton. Here was a car which, built to a new conception of mechanical perfection, leapt at once into the world class and has led the automobile world ever since. The car at the left (which is still running) carried out an historic 15,000-mile reliability run between London and Glasgow. At the wheel is Claude Johnson, "the man who introduced Rolls to Royce." Driving AX205 is the Hon. C. S. Rolls himself. Below is a typical scene from the same year's Isle of Man T.T., in which two races, for cars of different sizes in full touring trim, were held simultaneously. Highest speed was that of E. Courtis, on a Rover, who averaged 28·8 m.p.h. over the twisting and mountainous course. These were primarily sporting events, but they also demonstrated to the general public the practicability of the motor-car.

1908 MRS. PATRICK CAMPBELL. Married to Captain Campbell at the age of nineteen, Mrs. Patrick Campbell, seen in "Electra" in the top picture, first made her name in Pinero's "The Second Mrs. Tanqueray." One of the great tragic actresses of her generation, she also achieved a notable success as Eliza Doolittle in Shaw's "Pygmalion," and gained further laurels when making her film debut in "Rip Tide" in 1934 at the age of sixty-eight.

1908 GAIETY GIRLS. Under George Edwardes's management, the Gaiety Theatre was the headquarters of London musical comedy in the early years of the twentieth century. The productions, as regards both words and music, proving somewhat insipid after their Gilbert and Sullivan predecessors, Edwardes recruited to his casts a number of young ladies whose charm and beauty were soon famous. Below we see the 1908 bevy, who were (left to right), back row: Margaret Webster, Irene Warren, Tessie Hackney, Pattie Wells, Enid Leonhardt; front row: Marie Dean, Kitty Lindley, Edith Lee, May Sarony.

1908 SALE-TIME IN PICCADILLY. To modern eyes it may seem that the art of window dressing, as represented by the above picture of a famous London store, had not progressed very far. But the goods were there, and at prices which shoppers could afford, and shopping had become one of the chief delights of the feminine community in the days before the all-electric house, the radio and the films, and other similar diversions.

1908 SIR THOMAS LIPTON, BART. Here we have an embodiment of the cliché, "Poor Boy Makes Good." Born in 1850 of poor Irish parents in Glasgow, he started as an errand boy, became a millionaire through the vast chain of grocer's shops which he created and was a personal friend of Edward VII. A famous yachtsman, he spent a fortune in trying to bring back to England the America's Cup, but not one of his famous series of "Shamrock" yachts ever quite succeeded.

155

1908 MRS. LAMBERT CHAMBERS AT WIMBLEDON. Without a doubt the greatest woman player of lawn tennis up to the time of Suzanne Lenglen, Mrs. Lambert Chambers is here shown playing at Wimbledon when at the height of her powers. She first won the Women's Singles in 1903 and six times thereafter. She was eventually beaten in a memorable match by Suzanne Lenglen in 1919.

1908 JACK JOHNSON. World heavy-weight champion from 1908 until 1915, the American negro, Jack Johnson, was ill-conducted, aggressive and quarrelsome, and a merciless opponent. But he was also one of the greatest fighters of all time, and this picture shows how well equipped physically he was for his chosen trade. At the age of thirty-seven he was counted out in the twenty-sixth round of a sensational fight with Jess Willard at Havana, Cuba.

1908 MARATHON SENSATION. Possibly the highlight of every series of modern Olympic Games is the Marathon race of 26 miles 385 yards. In 1908, when the Games were held in London, the first competitor to reach the Stadium at Shepherd's Bush from the start at Windsor was an Italian waiter, Dorando. The race had been run in grilling heat, and Dorando collapsed a few yards from the winning-post. Helped to his feet by frenzied spectators and officials, he finished the course as shown in the dramatic picture below, but the stewards had no option but to disqualify him and award the race to the second runner home, the American J. J. Hayes.

1908 GIANT FLIP-FLAP. The "Entente Cordiale" with France was cemented by an Anglo-French Exhibition at the White City, London, in 1908. Among the diversions provided for the patrons was the giant flip-flap (left). Over eight million people attended the exhibition, which, unlike most other international exhibitions, finished up with a small financial profit.

1909 ROYAL DERBY VICTORY. The Derby was won for the first and only time by a reigning sovereign when King Edward VII's horse, Minoru, won the race in 1909. This very popular success had been preceded by two victories when he was Prince of Wales (1896, Persimmon and 1900, Diamond Jubilee). King Edward VII took a keen interest in all sport and entertainment.

1909 RASPUTIN THE MONK. A simple Russian peasant, Rasputin, born in 1871, apparently possessed remarkable powers of healing and secured entry to the Tsar's court by his alleged cure of the Tsarevich dying from haemophilia. Thereby he won complete domination over the Tsarina and had become by this date a great political power in Russia, as is shown by this picture of him seated while two high-ranking nobles stand respectfully behind him. By 1916 he was a menace to Imperial Russia and was assassinated by a group of patriotic nobles.

1909 ABDUL HAMID DEPOSED. Sultan Abdul Hamid of Turkey reigned from 1876 till 1909. He was more generally execrated by Britons than any other foreign ruler, his Bulgarian massacres of 1876 and subsequent Armenian massacres making his name notorious for cold-blooded cruelty. His overthrow in 1909 was achieved by the "Young Turks," one of whom, Mustafa Kemal, was later to become dictator of Turkey and to institute many beneficial and lasting reforms.

1909 FIRST MAN TO REACH THE NORTH POLE. Seen here on his return, the American Robert E. Peary (1856-1920) reached the North Pole after twenty-six years devoted to Arctic research. His claim was disputed by a rival named Cook, but is now universally accepted. An American naval officer, he was promoted to be rear-admiral in 1911. He had made previous attempts to reach the North Pole in 1902 and 1905, and although unsuccessful, on each occasion he had penetrated farther north than any previous explorer.

1910 CREATOR OF THE SCOUTS. Sir Robert Baden-Powell (later Lord Baden-Powell) achieved celebrity twice over: first as the successful commander of the garrison of Mafeking; and later as the founder of the Boy Scout (1908) and Girl Guide (1910) organizations. "Scouting" rapidly spread all over the world, and the biennial jamborees became international gatherings. Lord Baden-Powell received his peerage, a barony, in 1929 and died in 1941.

1910 HISTORIC SOUTH AFRICAN GROUP. The constitution of the Union of South Africa was enacted by the British Parliament in 1910. The members of the first Union Cabinet are pictured below: Louis Botha (seated in the centre) became the first Prime Minister; Jan Smuts (standing, extreme left), James Hertzog (standing, second from right) and Daniel Malan (standing, extreme right) were all future Prime Ministers. The photograph thus includes every premier of the Union so far.

1911 STINIE MORRISON IN THE DOCK. The trial of Stinie Morrison at the Old Bailey in March, 1911, on the charge of murdering Leon Beron on the morning of New Year's Day was one of the most singular and enthralling of murder trials and evoked great public interest. Both Morrison and his alleged victim were Jewish immigrants from Eastern Europe living in the East End of London and belonging to the professional criminal class. The evidence produced revealed, amid a tissue of perjuries, an extraordinary picture of this submerged society and illustrated the saying that "one-half of the world does not know how the other half lives." The court was packed throughout the trial. The picture on the right shows Stinie Morrison standing in the dock, looking over a group of barristers towards the judge; above the barristers are seated the jury in various attitudes of concentration. The trial reached its conclusion on the evening of 15 March. Mr. Richard Muir, the counsel for the defence, finished speaking at 7 p.m. and the summing up of Mr. Justice Darling took an hour. The jury was absent for only thirty minutes and returned with a verdict of "guilty." When sentence had been passed the hopelessness of the prisoner found expression in the words, "I do not believe there is a God in Heaven." Owing to a trace of dubiousness in the evidence, however, the sentence was commuted to one of imprisonment for life.

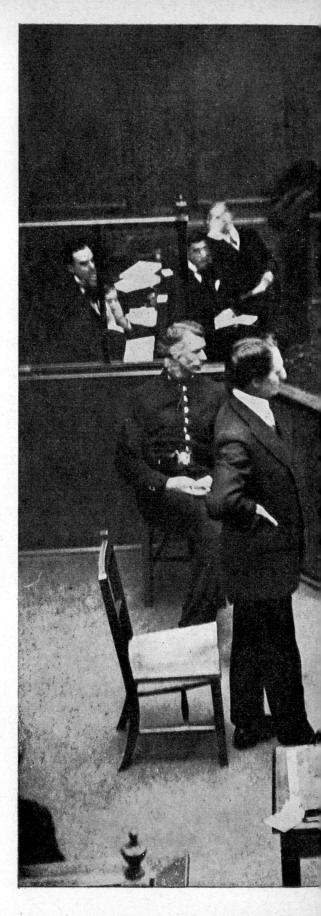

1911 EARLY FILM. D. W. Griffith was the first film-director to demonstrate the possibilities of the film (silent until the late twenties). Mary Pickford and Arthur Johnson are seen above in a typically melodramatic scene from a film directed by him.

1911 SECOND MAN TO SWIM THE CHANNEL. The Channel was first swum in 1875 by Captain Matthew Webb, but his feat was not repeated until 1911, when Thomas W. Burgess (seen below) swam from England to France in 22 hr. 35 min.

1911 THE PRINCE OF WALES WITH W. G. GRACE. This photograph, showing the young Prince of Wales posing with W. G. Grace, illustrates the prestige which W. G. had brought to himself and the game which he had adorned for so many years. Though sixty-three when the picture was taken, the "Grand Old Man" still retains much of the alert eye and upright bearing of his youth (see page 97).

1911 CORONATION OF KING GEORGE V. King Edward
VII died in May, 1910, and was succeeded by George V.
After the Coronation in June, 1911, the new King and Queen
toured South London, and are here seen at St. George's Circus.

1912 KING GEORGE V IN NEPAL. Six months after his coronation in London, King George was crowned Emperor of India at Delhi, the ancient capital of the Great Moguls, to which the seat of the Viceroy's government had been transferred from Calcutta a short time previously. George V was the first and the last British sovereign to celebrate his coronation in India. A number of important announcements were made, including the provision of grants for educational purposes and the eligibility of Indian troops for the Victoria Cross. The capital of India was transferred from Calcutta to historic Delhi, and the Partition of Bengal, highly unpopular with many Indians, was ended. After his coronation the King visited Nepal. This kingdom, which forms a long narrow strip along the Himalayan frontier of India, was never a part of the British Indian Empire, but its warlike sons supplied some of the finest troops of the British Indian Army —the Gurkhas. It now has representation by ambassadors to the Governments of Great Britain, the United States and India. In this picture the King is seen (with arm extended) at the successful conclusion of a tiger hunt.

168

1912 TRAGIC MAIDEN VOYAGE. On 15 April the White Star liner "Titanic," the largest and finest ship then afloat, while steaming at full speed across the Atlantic on her maiden voyage, struck the submerged part of an iceberg and went to the bottom. Of the 2,224 people on board 1,513 were lost. This tragedy, which shocked the whole world, led to considerably improved safety precautions at sea; these included regulations concerning lifeboats and lifebelts and the institution of the International Ice Patrol, charged with the duties of logging and watching icebergs in the North Atlantic. The picture on the left shows the "Titanic" leaving Belfast harbour shortly before her single fateful voyage.

1912 THE SCOTT ANTARCTIC EXPEDITION. The British Antarctic Expedition, under the Command of Captain Robert Falcon Scott, left England in 1910. On 18 January, 1912, Scott and four others reached the South Pole but found that the Norwegian explorer, Amundsen, had attained the goal from another starting point a month earlier. The party perished on its return journey. Petty Officer Evans was the first to succumb to the hardships. Then the sick Captain Oates walked to his death in the snow so that he would no longer be a burden to his companions. The surviving three, Dr. Wilson, Lt. Bowers and Captain Scott, were caught in a blizzard and perished within 11 miles of the provision base that would have saved them. Scott's diaries have become a classic of heroic endeavour. The picture on the right shows Captain Scott writing in his diary at the outset of the expedition. That below shows the party at the Pole. Left to right: Dr. Wilson, Lt. Bowers, Petty Officer Evans, Captain Scott, Captain Oates.

1912 TWO GREAT STAGE PER-
SONALITIES. Though there
could not have been a greater contrast in the theatrical activities of
Ellen Terry, the sensitive dramatic
actress, and Marie Lloyd, the mis-
tress of music-hall comedy, they
yet had certain points in common;
both were greatly beloved by British
audiences, and both reached the
zenith of their fame in the spacious
days of the Edwardian era. Ellen
Terry (1848-1928) was born into a
theatrical family and first appeared
on the stage at the age of eight. In
1878 she became leading lady at the
Lyceum under Sir Henry Irving's
management and appeared in his
numerous Shakespearean productions. Shaw designed for her a part
in "Captain Brassbound's Conver-
sion." Marie Lloyd (1870-1922)
popularized songs containing lines
which have become embedded in
common speech, such as "Everything in the garden's lovely" and "I
do like to be beside the seaside."
The picture on the left shows Ellen
Terry as Portia, while below, Marie
Lloyd is seen rehearsing a number.

1912 CRICKETING PRINCE. Kumar Shri Ranjitsinhji, popularly known as "Ranji," was one of the great cricketers of the early years of the century. A batsman of outstanding genius, he did perhaps more than anyone else to develop the modern style with its rapid footwork. After gaining his blue for cricket at Cambridge, he joined the Sussex county team (1895). He had the highest English batting average in 1896 and 1900; in the latter year he scored over 3,000 runs with an average of 87. In a county match against Middlesex he made 202 when the next highest score on his side was 17. In 1907 he succeeded to the chieftainship of his Indian state as Jam Sahib of Nawanagar. He died in 1933.

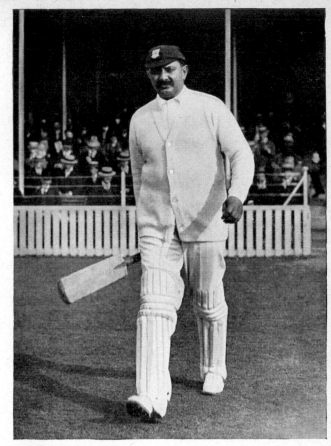

1912 ALL-ROUND ATHLETE. Charles Burgess Fry, born in 1872, who is shown left, has been one of the outstanding British athletes of all time. At Oxford University, where he took a first-class honours degree, he was soccer and cricket captain and President of the University Athletic Club. He played for England as a full international at association football, and many times in cricket Tests, being England's captain in the "triangular" Tests of 1912. For some years he held the world long-jump record. A superb batsman, who shares with Bradman the distinction of making centuries in six consecutive innings, he often partnered Ranjitsinhji as Sussex opening batsman, and later played for Hampshire. He was a close personal friend of "Ranji" and his secretary at the League of Nations.

172

1912 OIL KING AND HIS WIFE. John D. Rockefeller (1839-1937) founded in 1870 the Standard Oil Company, which gradually secured control of practically the whole petroleum industry of the U.S.A. He became the richest man of his day, and in 1890 began to organize the system of world-wide philanthropy now comprehended in the Rockefeller Foundation. The above picture shows Rockefeller and his wife arriving at Cleveland, Ohio.

1912 ROYAL CHILDREN. This group of the royal children taken while they were at Balmoral shows, left to right: Prince George (the late Duke of Kent), Prince Albert (King George VI), Princess Mary (Princess Royal), the Prince of Wales (King Edward VIII and Duke of Windsor), Prince Henry (Duke of Gloucester).

KEY TO ABOVE PHOTOGRAPH

1. Harry Blake
2. Arthur Revell
3. Harry Stelling
4. Alice Tremayne
5. M. Broadfoote
6. Cinquevalli
7. George D'Albert
8. Charles Coborn
9. Harry Grattan
10. Wilkie Bard
11. Vesta Tilley
12. Arthur Prince
13. John Le Hay
14. Babs
15. Harry Claff
16. Beatie
17. G. H. Chirgwin
18. Billy Williams
19. Mary Law
20. Pavlova
21. Jack Marks
22. George Gray
23. George Leyton
24. Edwin Barwick
25. Herbert Darnley
26. Cecilia Loftus
27. Vasco
28. Fanny Fields
29. Cruickshank

30. Diana Hope
31. Fred Farren
32. Ida Crispi
33. James Stewart
34. Pipifax
35. Panlo
36. Charles Austin
37. Marie Kendall
38. Fred Curran
39. Alfred Lester
40. Novikoff
41. Percy Delevine
42. Harriet Vernon
43. David Devant
44. Harry Delevine
45. J. W. Rowley
46. Martin Adeson
47. Alexandra Dagmar
48. Mrs. Adeson
49. Harry Lauder
50. T. E. Dunville
51. Kate Carney
52. Harry Tate
53. Fred Emney
54. George Bastow
55. Joe Tennyson
56. Chas. Whittle
57. J. W. Tate
58. Clarice Mayne

59. Peggy Pryde
60. Tom Woottwell
61. Harry Champion
62. Minnie Duncan
63. Arthur Godfrey
64. George Robey
65. Gus Elen
66. Barclay Gammon
67. Albert Le Fre
68. Arthur Gallimore
69. James Finney
70. Lupino Lane
71. Chas. McConnell
72. Joe McConnell
73. Ed. E. Ford
74. Cliff Ryland
75. Irene Rose
76. Fred Kitchen
77. Florence Smithers
78. Arthur Lennard
79. Ryder Slone
80. My Fancy
81. Esta Stella
82. Gracie Whiteford
82(a) Tom Edwards'
　　　Dummy
83. Fred Sinclair
84. Seth Egbert
85. J. Alexandre

86. Harry Freeman
87. Albert Egbert
88. W. F. Frame
89. G. Hughes
90. Dave Carter
91. Elsie Finney
92. Billie Bint
93. Julia Macarte
94. Will Kellino
95. Jack Lorimer
96. Harry Weldon
97. George French
98. Emilie D'Alton
99. Ella Retford
100. Edmund Edmunds
101. Albert Edmunds
102. "Papa" Brown
103. Tom Stuart
104. Harry Randall
105. Marie Loftus
106. W. J. Churchill
107. Harry Webber
108. R. H. Douglass
109. La Pia
110. Florrie Forde
111. Florrie Gallimore
112. Edith Evelyn
113. Tom Clare
114. Ella Shields

115. Harry Ford
116. Flora Cromer
117. William Downes
118. Charles Langford
119. J. W. Wilson
120. Deane Tribune
121. Bob Leonard
122. Jennie Leonard
123. Cecilia Macarte
124. George Newham
125. Fred Latimer
126. Joe Boganny
127. Sydney James
128. Alf Lotto
129. Clara Lilo
130. Ernest Otto
131. Gus McNaughton
132. Fred McNaughton
133. Horace Wheatley
134. Arthur Rigby
135. Albert Athas
136. Carlton
137. Marriott Edgar
138. Lizzie Collins
139. F. V. St. Clair
140. Ada Cerito
141. Fred Herbert
142. W. Munro

1912 COMMAND PERFORMANCE. When Queen Victoria issued the first "command" for a theatrical performance at Windsor she set a fashion which her successors followed with enthusiasm. It was many years, however, before the Variety Stage attained such a dignity, and this picture shows the impressive array of talent gathered at the Palace Theatre, London, on 1 July, 1912, for the first Variety Command Performance in the presence of the late King George V and of Queen Mary. Perhaps no other period, before or since, has produced so many great stars in this particular sphere. The key below gives the names of all of them. Even today many of these names are well remembered. Anna Pavlova, peerless classical dancer of her day, was 27 years old, and already world-famous. George Robey, acclaimed as the "Prime Minister of Mirth," was nearly 43. Harry Lauder, already amassing a large fortune by singing Scottish songs of his own composition, was a year younger. Those old enough to have seen Paul Cinquevalli say with conviction that he was the greatest juggler of modern times. Two years after this performance he retired at the age of 55. All these, and more than a hundred others, contributed to a truly notable occasion.

1912 GERMAN DIPLOMAT. In order the more completely to deceive the British Government as to its ultimate and aggressive intentions, the German Government in 1912 appointed as its Ambassador to the Court of St. James's the Anglophile Prince Karl Max Lichnowsky (left). Of an amiable disposition, and sincerely desirous of improving Anglo-German relations, he was himself kept largely in the dark as to his country's real policy. During the First World War Lichnowsky published a pamphlet, "My British Embassy," in which he expressed friendship and admiration for Sir Edward Grey and other British statesmen, and entirely exonerated them from the charges of duplicity brought against them in the German press. As a result he was expelled from the Prussian Diet and took refuge in Switzerland. He returned to Germany and died in 1928.

1912 BRITISH REVIVALIST. "General" William Booth, the founder of the Salvation Army, started preaching at the age of fifteen. The Salvation Army developed out of an open-air mission in Whitechapel which had been actively at work for some years before it was given, in 1878, the name under which it spread all over the world. Booth presented religion in a guise designed to appeal to those whom the "indoor" religions did not reach—with uniforms, marching and music. He sometimes had hymns sung to the tunes of music-hall successes. He is seen below in the last year of his life. He died in 1912 at the age of 83.

1912–13 WARS IN THE BALKANS. In 1912 Bulgaria, Serbia and Greece formed an alliance for the purpose of partitioning amongst themselves the still considerable territory of Turkey in Europe. They declared war in the autumn. In 1913 they fell out over the division of the spoils and Bulgaria was attacked and defeated by Greece and Serbia. The upshot was that Turkey was confined to a small province near Constantinople, the three other belligerents secured increases of territory, and an independent Albania was created. Turkish infantry (above) and Bulgarian artillery (below) are depicted as they move up to the front.

1912 FIRST ALEXANDRA ROSE DAY. The ladies in the above photograph are selling roses outside the Hotel Cecil in the Strand, London. This may be reckoned the first, and one of the biggest, of what soon afterwards came to be called Flag Days.

1913 BATHING BELLES. The costumes worn by the group pictured below are an amusing reminder of how much clothing was then considered consistent with decorum for girls wishing to have a bathe. But the young ladies don't seem to mind!

1913 FASHION AT ASCOT. The lady in the above picture illustrates the height of fashion immediately before the First World War. The wartime activities of women delivered them not only from the enormous "picture" hat but also from the trailing skirt, but Ascot continues to this day a famous "fashion parade."

1913 ROYAL DIPLOMACY. Tension between Britain and Germany was growing steadily. In the tradition of his father, Edward the Peacemaker, King George V paid a state visit to his cousin, Kaiser Wilhelm II, with a view to improving relations between their countries. They are seen above during a ceremonial procession, but for all their personal amiability the rivalry of their nations was not to be stopped short of the war which was to break out during the succeeding year.

1913 PAST AND FUTURE OF AIR-TRAVEL. Balloon contests, such as that at Hurlingham, England (shown above), were popular with fashionable society. Balloons, however, with a long past behind them, had no future. That lay with powered craft such as Cody's waterplane (below). Colonel Samuel Franklin Cody, the first man in England to fly, was one of the many pioneers of flight who met death in one of their own machines. His speciality, on which he had worked in conjunction with the British Army authorities, was man-lifting box-kites. In 1908 he constructed his first successful flying machine, and was airborne in it for 27 minutes. In 1913, the year of his death, he was combining the box-kite with the biplane structure. An American by birth, he eventually became a naturalized British subject.

1914 TROUBLE OVER IRISH HOME RULE. In 1912 the British Liberal Government introduced a Home Rule Bill to give limited self-government to the whole of Ireland. The Bill was passed through the House of Commons but was delayed for three sessions by the House of Lords. During this period Northern Ireland threatened armed resistance to the Bill. The crisis was postponed by the outbreak of the First World War. The above photograph shows the then Prime Minister, Mr. H. H. Asquith, visiting Ireland during this critical period.

1914 PIONEER OF WOMEN'S EMANCIPATION. Mrs. Pankhurst founded the Women's Social and Political Union in 1903, but after failing in 1905 to secure from the Liberal Government a promise to give women the vote, directed her "suffragettes" into methods of violence. In 1913 she was sentenced to three years' penal servitude. In prison she went on hunger-strike, was released when her life was endangered thereby, re-arrested on recovery, and so on again and again. She is here seen being arrested outside Buckingham Palace in 1914.

1914 OPENING OF THE PANAMA CANAL. It is a curious coincidence that the Suez Canal was opened on the eve of the Franco-Prussian War and the Panama Canal on the eve of the First World War. Both projects had long been discussed. Prince Louis Napoleon wrote a pamphlet on the latter project in 1842 and Great Britain and America made a treaty on the subject in 1850. A French company commenced work on the canal in 1881 but abandoned it again eight years later. The finally successful work was undertaken by the American Government under Theodore Roosevelt in 1902 and completed in the presidency of Woodrow Wilson. The extent of the excavation was 220 million cu. yd. and the cost 460 million dollars. The official opening ceremony was on 15 August, 1914, and above a U.S. battleship is seen clearing the Gatun Locks by the barest possible margin soon afterwards.

1914 ASSASSINATION AT SARAJEVO. The real causes of the outbreak of the First World War were complex indeed, but the immediate cause was the assassination of the heir to the Austro-Hungarian throne, Archduke Franz Ferdinand, and his morganatic wife at Sarajevo, capital of Bosnia, by a Serb named Gavrilo Princip. Above, the Archduke and his wife are seen a few moments before they were shot; below, Princip, the student, is being arrested by the police. As a result Austria issued an ultimatum to Serbia which the latter found it impossible to accept. Russia backed Serbia, and Germany, Austria. The powers mobilized for war. Europe was divided into two armed camps and a gigantic conflict followed almost at once.

1914 OUTBREAK OF FIRST WORLD WAR. On 2 August, when Germany was already at war with Russia, Belgium rejected Germany's demand of a right of passage for the German armies invading France and appealed to Britain to assist her in defending her neutrality in accordance with the terms of the treaty of 1839. Sir Edward Grey, the Foreign Secretary, told the House of Commons that an ultimatum, due to expire at midnight on the following day, had been sent to Germany demanding her recognition of Belgian neutrality. Germany replied by invading Belgium on 4 August and Britain accordingly entered the war. Above and below are scenes of war fever in London (outside Buckingham Palace) and Berlin.

186

1914 BRITAIN AT WAR. Lord Kitchener was appointed Secretary of State for War on 5 August and immediately called for 100,000 volunteers "for three years or the duration of the war." The limitation to 100,000 was due to the fact that for some time to come it would be impossible to provide even that limited number with equipment. The outbreak of war thus found Britain still pursuing her traditional policy of keeping a small army as compared with those of her continental neighbours, though her navy was easily the largest in the world. The picture on the right shows a famous recruiting poster carrying a portrait of Kitchener. Below are seen some of the first recruits to Kitchener's Army drilling without uniforms; one is leading the unit's canine mascot.

1915 DARDANELLES CAMPAIGN. On 2 January, 1915, Russia, cut off from her Western Allies, made an urgent request for ammunition, the lack of which was gravely impairing the fighting efficiency of her huge armies. The most practicable route by which supplies could be got to Russia was via the Dardanelles, sealed by Turkey's entry into the war in October, 1914, on Germany's side. Winston Churchill, then First Lord of the Admiralty, suggested that the Straits be forced by a combined naval and military assault. The War Council decided on 13 January to force the Straits and occupy the Gallipoli peninsula which dominated them. This bold and sound idea was ruined by maladroit execution. The preliminary naval bombardment of the peninsula took place in February. On 28 March a naval group attempted to force the Straits but turned back after several of the ships had been sunk. It was not until nearly a month later (25 April) that the military assault was made with five divisions under the command of General Sir Ian Hamilton. By this time the Turks, well and truly alerted, had six divisions occupying strong defensive positions in the invasion area. The Allies managed, however, with heavy losses, to secure two tenuous beach-heads—one in the Cape Hellas area, the other near Gaba Tepe—but were unable, despite strenuous efforts, to extend them. Further reinforcements arrived in July. Hamilton used these to reinforce the Anzacs at Gaba Tepe and to make a fresh landing at Suvla Bay; it was planned that these two forces would by a combined attack carry Sari Bair, a craggy height commanding the narrows. That the plan failed was largely due to the lethargy of the Suvla Bay commanders, who allowed precious time to elapse until the negligible opposition had been substantially reinforced. In December, 1915, and January, 1916, Allied troops were evacuated from the peninsula. The picture shows Turkish shells bursting near the s.s. "River Clyde," which landed troops in the Cape Hellas area during the initial assault.

1916 EASTER WEEK REBELLION. The Irish Republican society Sinn Fein (Gaelic for "ourselves alone") was founded in 1900 by Arthur Griffith, and after a while attracted a considerable following. Much more extreme than the National Party led by John Redmond, it desired complete independence for Ireland and was violently anti-British in sentiment. In Easter week, 1916, it staged a rebellion in Dublin. The cargo of arms brought from Germany by Sir Roger Casement had been sunk before arrival, and the rebellion was a forlorn hope from the start. Nevertheless, it marked the beginning of the series of events that has led to Irish independence. Of the leaders of the rebellion all but one were executed, De Valera being spared because he was technically an American citizen. The picture on the right shows British soldiers on duty beside a heap of wreckage in a battered Dublin street.

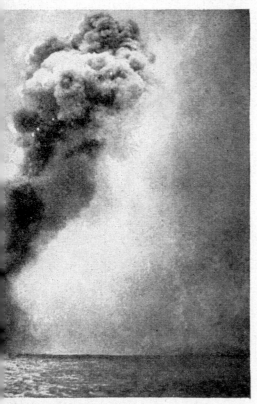

1916 THE BATTLE OF JUTLAND on 31 May, 1916, was the only occasion on which the grand fleets of Britain and Germany encountered one another. The battle may be termed indecisive. Germany's High Seas Fleet withdrew within the maze of its own minefield and the British Grand Fleet under Jellicoe refused to follow it. As Churchill wrote long afterwards, "Jellicoe was the only man on either side who could have lost the war in one afternoon." The British Navy remained in control of the surface of the seas after the battle, as before it. Before the main fleets joined action the British battle-cruisers engaged the enemy and were severely handled. The picture (left) shows H.M.S. "Queen Mary" (right) blowing up, and H.M.S. "Lion" (left) being shelled. The battle-cruiser squadron was commanded by Vice-Admiral Sir David (later Earl) Beatty.

191

1917 AIR-RAID WARNING. There were in all 109 German air raids over British soil in the First World War. Fifty-two were undertaken by Zeppelins in 1915-16. In 1917-18 the raids were carried out by planes. Total British casualties by air raids for the whole war were 1,400 killed. The primitive system of air-raid warning which employed a touring police-car is illustrated above.

1917 FAMOUS RATION CARD. A Ministry of Food and food-rationing were not instituted in Britain till December, 1916, more than halfway through the war, and both were ended a few months after its conclusion. The food-rationing was, in essentials, the same as that employed in the Second World War. The King's meat-ration card, exactly similar to all others, is shown on the left.

192

1916 WOMEN IN WAR. The enormous demands on the nation's man-power made by the fighting services provided both an opportunity and a challenge to the women of Britain. The urgency of the demand overcame prejudice and thousands of women volunteered to fill men's jobs in offices and factories, on the land, as bus conductresses (right), transport drivers and postwomen, and in munition work of all kinds. Some even worked as navvies (below). Without their efforts the armies could not have been maintained in men or materials. As a result it became widely accepted that women had earned some of the rights hitherto reserved to men, and when, in 1918, this was recognized in a Bill giving votes to women over the age of 30 it was overwhelmingly supported by all parties in Parliament. The public conscience had changed since those pre-war days when the efforts of the suffragettes had been so strongly condemned on every hand.

1916 GERMAN GAS ATTACK ON THE EASTERN FRONT. Immediately on the outbreak of war two Russian armies advanced into East Prussia. The Germans under Hindenburg, outnumbered though they were, defeated the Russian armies separately and drove them out of East Prussia with the loss of a quarter of a million men. The Allies in the West had great hopes of the Russian "steam-roller," but inferior generalship, poor supply organization and isolation from the West (which the Dardanelles expedition failed to rectify) led to a series of military failures in 1915. Some success was achieved in 1916, but at a price of enormous losses in men which finally sapped Russia's moral strength and led to complete collapse.

1916 READY FOR A GAS ATTACK.
Poison-gas was introduced in the First World War by the Germans but the Allies were quick to retaliate in like form. It was first used in April, 1915, against the French and Canadians and was in itself successful though the Germans failed to exploit it. The Allies quickly produced protective measures against gas and soon every soldier had his respirator. Right, Australian troops on the Western Front are shown ready for a gas attack.

1916 ZEPPELIN DOWN IN THE
SEA. Air raids on Britain by German Zeppelins were numerous during the early part of the war. As air defences improved, and particularly after the invention of the incendiary bullet for guns in aeroplanes, the cost in Zeppelin casualties became prohibitive, and thereafter the Germans used mainly aeroplanes. Several Zeppelins were shot down in flames over land, memorably those at Cuffley and Potter's Bar, Middlesex. Many more, as the one seen below, fell into the sea and were completely lost.

1917 ALLIED TANKS ATTACK ACROSS NO-MAN'S-LAND. This dramatic picture, taken from a German trench, shows how effectively the tank was solving the problem of attack. Even before 1916 the power of defence, resting on wire entanglements, complex trench systems and the machine-gun nest, had so outstripped the power of offence that advances by either side of a few miles were won only at the cost of fearsome losses. It is possible that had the tank not been invented by the British, a condition of stalemate might have been perpetuated on the Western

196

Front. A few experimental tanks were tried out on the Somme in 1916, but the first real tank battle was at Cambrai in 1917 when they achieved so brilliant a success that the Allies were quite unprepared to exploit it. Badly used tactically, the tank was dismissed by the Germans as of little value; but by 1918 the Allies had developed a technique, and the tank, which could crush down wire, roll over trenches and was impervious to machine-gun fire, proved itself a war-winning weapon to which the Germans failed to find an answer in time to prevent the Allied break-through.

1917 ALLENBY ENTERING JERUSALEM. Allied to Germany, the Turks attacked
the Suez Canal early in 1915, and the early operations of the British Army
in Egypt were directed towards protecting the canal, which was vital to the communications of the British Empire. However, the campaign developed into a general
onslaught on the Turkish Empire, and in 1917 British forces captured Jerusalem
(their commander, General Allenby, is here seen entering the city) and the Turks
were nearly exhausted. Allenby was greatly helped by the revolt of the Arabs, who,
aroused and led by Colonel T. E. Lawrence, harried Turkish communications.

198

1917 WAR IN THE AIR. By 1917 air warfare had made great advances on both sides. As the above photograph of a British patrol returning to its airfield at St. Omer shows, formation tactics were now in use. In the war's early days the Allies, who were behind the Germans in the development of air warfare, were limited to the use of aircraft for reconnaissance, but with improved and specialized aircraft the Royal Flying Corps now had fighters and bombers as well. The Germans had begun elementary strategic bombing—the bombing of enemy war industries and communications—in 1915, but the British had no suitable planes with which to retaliate until 1917. The great increase in the size of the air arm and the complexity of its operations led to the formation of the Royal Air Force in April, 1918. Improvements in artillery were almost as spectacular. Numbers and sizes of guns and their use greatly increased. The long-range mobile howitzer made great strides and the picture below shows a British battery of heavy howitzers engaging a distant target.

1918

BLOCKSHIPS AT ZEEBRUGGE. The celebrated action on the night of 22 and 23 April (St. George's Day), 1918, which blocked the entrance to the submarine base at Zeebrugge on the Belgian coast, was only one episode in a far greater struggle. Germany's major naval effort during the First World War took the form of submarine warfare. By unrestricted sinkings the enemy aimed at bringing seaborne traffic to and from Britain to a standstill. Had they succeeded, and they very nearly did, Britain would have been unable to continue the war. The submarine campaign rose to its peak of success in 1917, when submarines sank 1,134 British ships with a tonnage of over 3,000,000. At one period one in four of the ships leaving British ports failed to return. The worst month was April, when 196 ships were lost. It was not until the introduction of the convoy system in May, 1917, supported by improved anti-submarine weapons, that the menace was largely overcome. These measures, however, dealt with submarines at sea. Early in 1918 it was decided to block the two ends of the Bruges canal at Ostend and Zeebrugge, and thus deny its use as a base to the flotilla of German submarines which by its location was a particular threat to British shipping in the English Channel and Western Approaches. The photograph on these pages was taken shortly after the raid on Zeebrugge and shows where the three old cruisers which acted as blockships were sunk. The first, the "Thetis," fouled a net and sank just outside the canal entrance, but the two following, "Intrepid" and "Iphigenia," were sunk well in the canal entrance. In the meantime a landing had been made from the cruiser "Vindictive" on the mole (seen in the background), with the object of capturing the enemy batteries and so diverting fire from the blockships. In addition, the viaduct connecting the mole with the shore had been destroyed by having an old submarine jammed between its piers and there blown up, thus preventing reinforcements reaching the mole. The simultaneous operation at Ostend was a failure, as the attacking force could not find the harbour entrance. The failure was, however, rectified in brilliant fashion in the following month.

201

1917 REVOLT IN RUSSIA. The move towards revolution in Russia began in the spring of 1917, and resulted from military disasters in the war against Germany (see page 194) and the deteriorating conditions at home. Disturbances began with strikes and rioting in Petrograd (now Leningrad), but were not serious until the issue was somewhat changed by the shooting down of 150 of the demonstrators by police and troops (above). As a result numbers of sympathetic troops went over to the strikers. From then on Socialist influence increased and the Revolution gained

momentum. Before long the Czar, who had by now been forced to abdicate, was arrested. In the picture, left, he is seen (second from right) while under arrest before being sent to Siberia, where with his family he was later assassinated by the Bolsheviks. In October the Bolsheviks under Lenin swept the moderates out of power and assumed it themselves. They at once made peace overtures to the Germans and the Treaty of Brest-Litovsk was signed (right) in March, 1918. For the next three years the Bolsheviks fought a fearful civil war, but by the death of Lenin in 1924 were firmly in power.

1917 TRENCH WARFARE ON THE WESTERN FRONT. These pictures give an impression of the life in the trenches on the Western Front. In wet weather the trench became a river of mud; some shelter was provided by crude dug-outs. On the firing-step a sentry (as above) would keep watch while other troops snatched a rest where they could find comfort. For four years the opposing armies viewed one another across the narrow no-man's-land which separated their front lines. The boredom of trench warfare was relieved only by attacks, patrols and raids, and the humour of the British soldier. Below, British troops are seen fixing bayonets in a communication trench preparatory to going into the front line for an attack.

1918 THE GREAT BREAK-THROUGH. This long line of Canadian reinforcements is supporting the great Allied advance which began with a French attack in July and a British attack in August led by 450 tanks. It was destined in four months to end the war. Victory came as a surprise, for earlier in the year the Germans, reinforced by the divisions released from the East by the collapse of Russia, made their last attempt to win in the West. They made substantial advances but extended themselves so far that they were unable to withstand the counter-stroke.

1918 FLANDERS MUD. The feature of the battlefields of Flanders which impressed itself most on the British soldier was the endless mud (above). Fought over back and forth for four years, the land became one vast quagmire for the attacker to pass.

1918 GERMAN FLEET SURRENDERS. The photograph (top right) taken from a ship of the British Grand Fleet off the Firth of Forth shows the German High Seas Fleet steaming northwards to surrender. After the surrender most of the vessels were interned in Scapa Flow, and in 1919, while the Allies argued what to do with them, their crews solved the problem by scuttling them.

1918 PÉTAIN HONOURED. Subsequent history gives a touch of irony to this picture (right) of Pétain, the defender of Verdun, about to receive his baton as a Marshal of France. Behind him stand Allied military chiefs (left to right) Joffre and Foch (France), Haig (Britain), Pershing (U.S.A.), Gillian (Belgium), Albrucci (Italy) and Haller (Poland). Weygand (France) is behind Haig.

206

1919 TREATY OF VERSAILLES. At the peace conference at Paris in 1919 the Allied leaders not only drew up the treaty with Germany, but also decided to attempt to establish an international body to prevent future wars. The men who had to grapple with these problems were (top left, right to left): Sonnino and Orlando (Italy), Lloyd George (Britain), Clemenceau (France), seen with Foch (Allied Commander-in-Chief) in London before the conference; and (above) President Wilson (U.S.A.), seen with King George V. All the leaders were under pressure of public opinion to take a stiff line with Germany, and if the Treaty of Versailles did not lay the foundation of a permanent world peace it was not entirely their fault. Inspired by the idealist Wilson, the Treaty began with the Covenant of the League of Nations, based on Wilson's famous Fourteen Points. He conceived it as the beginning of a new era in international relations. That his own country declined to join must be accounted a major cause of the League of Nations' failure when the testing time came. By the Treaty, Germany lost territory to France, Belgium, Denmark and Poland, including a corridor separating East Prussia from the rest of Germany, and was saddled with payment of fantastic reparations. The Rhineland was demilitarized. Germans were compelled to sign the Treaty in the Hall of Mirrors at Versailles in June, 1919, and it was brought into force six months later. Left, the assembled conference in progress.

1918 WOMEN GET THE VOTE. Six million women over the age of 30 were in 1918 given the vote and the right to be members of Parliament. The picture above shows three nurses casting their votes in the "khaki" election in December of the same year. It was not until 1919 that the first woman sat in Parliament. The same Act which gave women the vote gave full adult suffrage to the male population and altogether produced eight million new voters.

1919 ARMISTICE DAY. Simple and austere, the Cenotaph in Whitehall formed the focus of the nation's deepest feelings about its 812,000 war dead. The picture (left) shows crowds paying their tribute after the memorial service held at the Cenotaph on the first anniversary of the end of the war. The original Cenotaph was built of wood to the design of Sir Edwin Lutyens for the 1919 Peace Procession. It was reconstructed in stone during the following year.

1919 TWO NOTABLE FLIGHTS: After the First World War the possibility of using the great advances made in military aviation for commercial purposes captured the imagination of airmen, and a number of important pioneer flights were made which foreshadowed the regular air routes of today. In June a crash landing (above) in Galway, Ireland, ended the first non-stop transatlantic flight, when John Alcock and Arthur Whitten Brown flew 1,950 miles from St. John's, Newfoundland, in just over sixteen hours. The picture below shows Ross Smith preparing for the first flight to Australia. His success in the same year won him a £10,000 prize offered by the Government of Australia. These flights were carried out in military aircraft, suitable civil types not yet being available, though in the same year the first regular air-mail and passenger service was started between London and Paris with civil planes. From that time onward progress was rapid.

1919 FIRST WOMAN M.P. Lady Astor was elected to Parliament for a Plymouth constituency following the succession of her husband, the previous member, to the peerage. She soon became known for her enthusiasm, independence of mind and gift of repartee. She was particularly active in the interests of women, and by the time she retired from Parliament in 1945 women had become firmly established in Parliamentary life.

1920 THE UNKNOWN WARRIOR. To the thousands of bereaved parents and widows who filed past the coffin the Unknown Warrior, lying among the nation's most illustrious dead, took on the identity of a son or husband. Unidentified by name or rank, his remains were taken from a grave in France and buried in Westminster Abbey on Armistice Day, 1920. King George V acted as one of the pallbearers. The picture below shows the coffin during the ceremonial lying-in-state in the Abbey.

1921　SCENE FROM A FAMOUS FILM. Probably the greatest genius in developing the film as an independent art-form was Charlie Chaplin, pictured above with Jackie Coogan in a scene from his film, "The Kid." Chaplin began work in films in 1913 and though he always appealed to an unsophisticated sense of humour, there was behind his fooling a wealth of careful characterization, and often a somewhat unexpected depth of philosophy or of shrewd comment on social affairs.

1921 GRAECO-TURKISH WAR. It was not until 1917 that Greece came into the First World War on the side of the Allies. As her share in the spoils of victory she was awarded the greater part of Thrace, a number of islands in the Aegean Sea, and the city of Smyrna and its surrounding district in Asia Minor. Dissatisfied, Greece sought to increase her territory by making war on Turkey. Nothing but disaster came to her forces. They advanced deep into Asia Minor, where they were defeated by Mustapha Kemal, later to become first President of the Turkish Republic. The Turks advanced into Smyrna and captured the city, most of which was later destroyed in a disastrous fire. In the subsequent treaty Greece lost all her territory in Asia Minor. The photograph (right) shows Greek cavalry crossing the River Gallus during the early, and successful, part of the campaign.

1922 RISE OF FASCISM. The Italian Fascist movement had been founded in 1919 by Benito Mussolini. Its mainspring was an exaggerated patriotism and belief in the importance of the State as opposed to the individual, and a violent opposition to Communism. The "squadristi" of the Fascist Party—armed bands of ex-servicemen, youths and a few older men—had frequent clashes with the Communists in the industrial areas from 1920 to 1922. By then the Fascists had gained many adherents and their Congress that year felt strong enough to demand that Mussolini be made head of the Government. In October, a motley crowd of Fascists marched on Rome (Mussolini himself took the less heroic course of going by train) and the King reacted sympathetically to their arrival. A few days later Mussolini (in centre, in civilian clothes) and his supporters marched to the Palace to be received by the King, who appointed him prime minister. Before long he was dictator. Already democracy had fallen in a nation which only four years before had been among the victors in a war ostensibly fought "to make the world safe for democracy."

215

1922 END OF THE IRISH TROUBLES. The Easter rebellion in Dublin in 1916 (see page 190) and the consequent British measures were followed by a period of relative quiet during which the efforts of the British Government to negotiate a settlement seemed likely to have some success. These hopes were disappointed in 1918, when the passing of the Military Service Bill (which applied to Ireland, though it was never enforced there) once more inspired an anti-British outburst. In the 1918 election eighty-three Sinn Feiners were elected. Refusing to go to London, they promptly formed themselves into a National Assembly (Dail) and proclaimed Ireland an independent republic. Soon the more belligerent members of the movement began a sporadic campaign against the Irish constabulary, which led eventually to a general campaign of terrorism and arson against anti-Republican elements, the police, Black and Tans (an auxiliary police force) and even the regular military forces. Only small Republican forces were involved but their guerrilla tactics were most successful. The Dail had meanwhile gone underground, but in the election of 1921 (held under a new Act passed at Westminster in 1920) the Republicans were again victorious, and the British Government, which had been strongly criticized for its repressive policy, was forced to seek an agreement. The Republicans eventually came to terms and the Irish Free State with Dominion status was founded. This status did not satisfy the more ardent Republicans. A split in the Sinn Fein Party resulted, and civil war broke out in 1922 between the ardent Republicans and those in favour of the new constitution. This picture shows an incident during the civil war at the Four Courts, Dublin, where it began. The war went on until 1923, though by then the Dail had accepted the new constitution.

1923 DERBY VICTORY. One of the most popular British jockeys between the two World Wars was Steve Donoghue, and the shout "Come on Steve" was frequently heard on the racecourse. This picture shows Steve Donoghue on Papyrus being led in after winning the Derby. In 1920 he rode 143 winners, and between 1915 and 1925 he won the Derby six times, creating a record which beat that of Fred Archer and which remains unbeaten to this day.

1923 SCREEN'S GREAT LOVER. One of the most popular films showing in 1923 was "The Four Horsemen of the Apocalypse," in which Rudolph Valentino first appeared on the screen. His physical charms and the powerfully romantic parts he portrayed caused a considerable cult among women to grow up around him. When he died suddenly in 1926 his funeral was attended by a vast crowd, largely composed of hysterical women.

1923 ROYAL HONEYMOON. In April, 1923, the Duke of York, second son of King George V, married Lady Elizabeth Bowes-Lyon, daughter of the Earl of Strathmore. After the wedding in Westminster Abbey they spent the first part of their honeymoon at Polesden Lacey in Surrey, where this picture was taken.

1923 BEGINNING OF NAZISM. The Nazi party began in Munich as a small group which crystallized out of the political melting-pot following the German revolution of 1918. Like its Fascist counterpart in Italy it was violently anti-Communist, and in addition was anti-Semitic. Its nationalism was expressed notably in denunciation of the Treaty of Versailles. The group attracted a number of ex-soldiers, including Adolf Hitler, an Austrian who had had an undistinguished career in the German Army. But his personality and enthusiasm obtained for him the leadership of the group, and in 1923, with the assistance of a number of German ex-officers, including Gen. Ludendorff, former German Army Chief of Staff, he attempted a "coup d'état" at Munich. A burst of machine-gun fire quickly dispersed the revolutionaries, and as a result of his failure Hitler spent a short time in prison. There he recorded his political philosophy in his book "Mein Kampf." This picture, taken shortly before the Munich "putsch," shows (left to right) Pernet, Weber, Frick, Kriebel, Ludendorff, Hitler, Bruckner, Röhm and Wagner, all pioneer National Socialists.

1924 FIRST LABOUR GOVERNMENT. Ramsay MacDonald formed the first Labour Government in Britain in 1924, thirty-two years after Keir Hardie had entered Parliament as the first Labour member. Post-war troubles had greatly increased support for the British Labour Party, but unlike the new movements in Italy and Germany the Labour Movement was rooted deep in British history. It was socialist, but it was also firmly wedded to constitutional parliamentary methods. The 1924 Labour Government was, however, a minority government at the mercy of the Liberals, and lasted less than a year. The picture shows (left to right), front row: W. Adamson, Lord Parmoor, Philip Snowden, Lord Haldane, J. Ramsay MacDonald, J. R. Clynes, J. H. Thomas, A. Henderson; second row: C. P. Trevelyan, S. Walsh, Lord Thomson, Lord Chelmsford, Lord Olivier, Noel Buxton, J. Wedgwood, V. Hartshorn, T. Shaw; back row: S. Webb, J. Wheatley, F. W. Jowett.

221

1925 EMPIRE EXHIBITION.

In 1924 a giant exhibition was held at Wembley, a suburb of London, at which all aspects of life, culture, produce and trade from all parts of the British Empire were illustrated on a lavish scale. Left, King George V and Queen Mary enjoying a ride on the Canadian Pacific miniature railway, and below the reopening of the exhibition by the King for its second season. This ceremony took place in the great Empire Stadium which, while the exhibition was on, was the scene of a wild-west rodeo at which bronco-busting and steer roping were prominently featured. After the exhibition the stadium was purchased by a company formed for that purpose, and has become Britain's most famous arena for important sporting events, such as the final tie for the Football Association Challenge Cup.

1925 FIRE AT MADAME TUSSAUD'S. This famous exhibition of waxwork figures representing celebrities of all kinds, both past and present, was founded in London by a Swiss woman in 1802. A great fire destroyed the exhibition in 1925, but it was rebuilt and, after a century and a half, is still a favourite place of entertainment for Londoners. The picture shows firemen vainly fighting the flames.

1925 BROADCASTING BECOMES POPULAR. By 1925 over a million wireless receiving sets were in use in Britain. Broadcasting had begun at the end of 1922 and in three years had demonstrated many of its potentialities. This picture shows Sir Walford Davies broadcasting. His inimitable radio talks on music set a standard in the technique of broadcasting, and gave an indication of the educational possibilities of radio. His "studio audience" is a noteworthy feature.

1925 SIGNING THE LOCARNO PACT. A series of international agreements, drawn up at Locarno in Switzerland and signed in London (as seen above), heralded, it was hoped, a new era of peace in Western Europe. The leading parts in the negotiations were played by the British Foreign Secretary, Austen Chamberlain, and the German Chancellor, Gustav Stresemann. By the treaties the chief Western nations, including Germany, provided guarantees against aggression and agreed to arbitrate on differences. As a result Germany was in 1926 admitted to the League of Nations. The Allied occupation of the Rhineland continued for a time but British forces were withdrawn in 1929, and all other Allied forces the next year. Below, British Tommies, evidently in high spirits, are seen leaving Cologne.

1925 RAILWAY CENTENARY. The Stockton to Darlington railway was opened in 1825, and this 26¾-mile-long line, which established George Stephenson as the leading railway engineer, had the first public passenger-carrying steam train in the world, with a locomotive most appropriately called "Locomotion No. 1." The centenary was celebrated by running over the old route a train said to be a replica of the original one. The picture, right, shows the centenary train drawing into Stockton station. The coal trucks are filled with enthusiasts in early nineteenth-century costume, with "George Stephenson" plainly visible on the footplate. The original intention was to haul the trains by means of horses, and in spite of the "centenary train" it is stated on apparently good authority that the early passenger coaches were similar in appearance to stage coaches of the period and were horse-drawn for the first eight years.

1925 OPENING OF KEN WOOD. A large addition to London's open spaces was made when, as seen left, King George V opened as a public park over a hundred acres of Ken Wood. This fine woodland with its splendid pines and oaks, adjoining Hampstead Heath, contains a mansion rebuilt by Robert Adam in the eighteenth century. It later came into the possession of the Earl of Iveagh, who left the house with its valuable collection of paintings, particularly of the British, French and Dutch Schools of the eighteenth and nineteenth centuries, and the park, to the nation on his death in 1927. The whole area which he bequeathed amounts to nearly 200 acres.

1925 WAR IN MOROCCO. After the First World War the Riff tribes of Morocco fought hard for independence, and it was not until France and Spain joined forces in 1925 that they finally quelled the tribesmen. Above, sharpshooters, hard to spot against the hillside, are in action in Spanish Morocco.

1925 PRINCELY AMBASSADOR. The Prince of Wales made a number of lengthy tours abroad to foster good relations between the mother country and other parts of the Commonwealth and with foreign nations. His popularity was enormous. Below, he meets an African chief during his South African visit of 1925.

1926 INCIDENT IN THE GENERAL STRIKE. The astonishing thing about Britain's General Strike (see page 25) was not the violence but the lack of it. Despite the inevitable bad feeling between strikers and volunteers endeavouring to keep essential services going, incidents such as that shown above where police are running to break up a fracas at the Elephant and Castle, London, were remarkably infrequent. Note the special police enrolled for the emergency.

1926 ROYAL ENTRY AT WIMBLEDON. To King George VI belongs the distinction, when Duke of York, of being the only member of the Royal Family who has played in an all-England tennis tournament at Wimbledon. In 1926, partnered by his equerry, Louis Greig, he entered the men's doubles, but was defeated by experienced opponents. At this time the Duke was beginning to earn the sobriquet of the Industrial Prince from the great interest he was showing in the factories and workshops throughout the country, coupled with real knowledge.

1926 BIRTH OF PRINCESS ELIZABETH. This picture shows Queen Mary
nursing her first grandchild, the baby Princess Elizabeth, who was born
on 21 April. The new princess immediately began to share the popularity which
the British people accorded her parents, the Duke and Duchess of York, and every
new development in her life and welfare was carefully noted by an interested
public. That she might one day be heir to the throne did not seem in the least
probable at that time; she was a general favourite entirely "in her own right."

1927 ROYAL VISIT TO CANBERRA. The new Parliament House at Canberra was opened by the Duke of York when he visited Australia with the Duchess in 1927. Though provision for a new federal capital had been made when Australia became a united Commonwealth in 1901, building was not completed and the Federal Parliament did not meet there until 1927.

1927 FIRST SOLO TRANSATLANTIC
FLIGHT. On the morning of 20 May,
1927, a young civil air-line pilot, Charles
Lindbergh, took off in his monoplane,
"Spirit of St. Louis," from a New York
airfield. Just 33½ hours later, and after covering 3,600 miles, he landed at Le Bourget
airfield, outside Paris, the first solo flier
of the Atlantic. He was greeted by crowds
of people hysterical in their enthusiasm.
Later he flew on to Croydon, and right he
is seen facing equally enthusiastic crowds
from the control tower shortly after his
landing. His flight won him not only international prestige but a prize of 25,000
dollars, and the British Air Force Cross
amongst other decorations. He was to
figure again prominently and tragically in
world news when in 1932 his child was
kidnapped and later was found murdered.

234

1927 WORLD TITLE FIGHT. One of the most controversial incidents in the history of professional boxing occurred in the Dempsey-Tunney fight in Chicago in 1927. After having begun the count on Tunney, who had been floored by a terrific blow from Dempsey, the referee broke off to order Dempsey to a neutral corner. He then began to count anew from "one." Tunney was up again before "ten," having been down for an equivalent of fourteen or fifteen. Tunney went on to win on points over ten rounds and thus retained the world heavy-weight title, having first challenged and defeated Dempsey (also on points) the previous year. Both Tunney and Dempsey rank high in the annals of boxing history; the former was perhaps the more accomplished boxer, the latter the more powerful fighter. Dempsey had held the world title since 1919, and Tunney retired in 1928 while still the undefeated world-champion.

1927 BRITISH SCHNEIDER TROPHY VICTORY. Flying at an average speed of 281 m.p.h. (astonishing for those days), Flight-Lieut. Webster won the Schneider Trophy for Great Britain at Venice. This picture shows Webster's seaplane about to be launched for a practice flight. Britain was also successful in 1929 and 1931 and thus won the trophy outright. All three victorious aircraft were designed by R. J. Mitchell, and they hold important places in the ancestry of his greatest aircraft, the "Spitfire." The Schneider Trophy was competed for eleven times between 1913 and 1931, being won on five occasions by Britain.

1927 LAND SPEED RECORD. In this year H. O. D. Segrave, driving the car pictured above, created a world's land speed record of 203 miles an hour at Daytona Beach, Florida. Losing the record to Campbell in 1928, he regained it in 1929 at 231 miles an hour. Britain has retained this record ever since.

1927 GREYHOUND RACING ARRIVES. Racing with greyhounds is an old-established field-sport, but the introduction of the electric hare led to a new form of track racing, immensely popular from 1927 onwards with the betting fraternity. Below is shown a race at the opening meeting at the White City Stadium.

1928 THAMES TRAGEDY. In January a combination of spring tides and abnormal rain raised the level of the Thames at London to a remarkable height. The banks were burst at a number of places, the two worst instances being between Lambeth Bridge and Vauxhall Bridge. The surging waters poured into hundreds of basements. At Millbank ten people were trapped and drowned. In the Thames Valley many square miles of countryside were flooded and hundreds of houses isolated. The picture, right, shows temporary sandbagging piled along the river bank in London in an attempt to hold back the water.

1929 SCOUT JAMBOREE. From its small beginnings in 1908 the Boy Scout movement had by 1929 become a vast international organization established in over thirty nations and with a membership in the region of two millions. In this year, to celebrate the coming-of-age of scouting, a great jamboree was held at Birkenhead Park, attended by scouts from all over the world. This picture shows Lord Baden-Powell, founder of the movement, with the Prince of Wales, surrounded by scout leaders from many countries during the jamboree.

1929 LEAGUE OF NATIONS IN SESSION. One of the problems facing the young League of Nations was to bring into its organization those nations which for various reasons were not founder members. The first of these to join was Germany, which was admitted in 1926. The German Chancellor was then Dr. Stresemann, a man of liberal outlook, with an international prestige, and the principal architect of the scheme embodied in the Treaty of Locarno, 1925. This picture shows Stresemann addressing the League Assembly shortly before his death in 1929. He had won the Nobel Peace Prize for 1926.

1929 BRITAIN ENDS AIRSHIP DEVELOPMENT. The R101 and her sister the R100 marked the end of British efforts to produce large airships. These two huge vessels were designed to carry 100 passengers at a speed of 70 miles an hour. The passengers were accommodated within the hull and were provided with cabins, a dining saloon and other comforts hitherto associated only with ocean liners. The two vessels were completed in 1929 and the next year the R101 began her maiden voyage to India. Disaster soon overtook her. In the early hours of 5 October, 1930, the great airship crashed and caught fire on a hillside near Beauvais, in Northern France, killing 48 people including Lord Thomson, the Air Minister. The R100 crossed the Atlantic and back but was dismantled after the R101 disaster. Above, R101 is moored at Cardington; below is seen all that was left after a disaster which shocked millions all over the world.

1929 STALIN CONSOLIDATES HIS POWER. Following the death of Lenin in 1924, power was won by Stalin after a fierce battle with Trotsky, who was driven into exile. Internecine strife, however, continued among the Bolsheviks and they were driven to "purge" their ranks of all dissidents and "deviationists." Originally the Bolsheviks (majority) had formed one wing of the Socialist party of which the Mensheviks (minority) formed the other and more moderate wing. In 1929 Stalin, alleging Menshevik intrigue, staged a mass trial of many of their leaders (seen above) and broke their power for ever. This and similar trials seemed of small moment to many people then but, in consolidating Stalin's power, they had, as everyone now realizes, immense far-reaching significance.

1932 DE VALERA IN POWER.
Having been saved by his American citizenship from execution after the 1916 Easter rebellion, Eamon de Valera was released from gaol in 1917 and at once elected Sinn Fein M.P. for East Clare. He refused to accept Cosgrave's compromise of the Irish Free State set up on a Dominion basis by the treaty of 1921, and it was as leader of the more extreme Feinna Fail that he won the election of 1932. He retained power until 1948, during which time Ireland became increasingly separatist and anti-British.

1932 DEATH OF A PRESIDENT.
The dramatic picture below shows the body of President Doumer of France, an old man of 75, being carried from the book exhibition at the Salon Rothschild in Paris, where he had been shot dead on 8 May. The assassin was a mad Russian named Gorguloff; his motives were not clear but were unlikely to have been political.

1932 EMPIRE STATESMEN AT OTTAWA. The Empire Conference at Ottawa
marked the end in Britain of the policy of "free trade," upon which British
prosperity had been nurtured under the very different economic conditions of
the nineteenth century. The world depression of 1929-32 and a refusal to desert
free trade had, rather than a policy of socialism, caused the British Labour Government of 1929 to collapse. The National Government which followed was committed
to a policy of protection and after the conference Britain and the Dominions adopted
a general tariff policy, but with "preference" for countries within the Empire.

244

1932 HISTORIC AIR FLIGHTS. In the early 1930s there were still many worlds for the airman to conquer. Among the pioneers was C. W. A. Scott, who in 1931 flew to Australia and back, and the next year made a record flight to Australia in just under nine days. (Right, Scott with his wife before his record flight.) In 1934 with Campbell Black he won the England-Australia air race in under three days. Also distinguished was Charles Kingsford-Smith (below), who was knighted in 1932. He made the first transpacific flight in 1928. In 1931 he made an air-mail flight from Australia to England and back. Four years later he disappeared while on a flight from England to Singapore. To the general public these flights were little more than sporting events, but they were of great importance in demonstrating what ordinary, and in many cases inexpensive, aircraft could be made to do in the hands of exceptionally skilled and determined pilots.

1933 LUXURY LINER ABLAZE. This remarkable aerial view
shows the giant French liner "L'Atlantique," 42,512
tons, ablaze in the English Channel. Fortunately no passengers
were aboard; the interior was gutted, and the hull badly damaged.

1933 NEW DOCKS AT SOUTHAMPTON. The facilities of
Southampton, Britain's main transatlantic port, were
inadequate for the growing size of ships. New docks were opened
in 1933. Below, large vessels are seen moored at the new quays.

1933 BURNING OF THE REICHSTAG. On the night of 27 February, 1933, the building of the Reichstag (German parliament) burst into flames and was burnt out as seen above. Hitler had become Chancellor in January but his party had lost seats at the previous election. Even before the fire was out, the Nazis were blaming the Communists for it and declaring their deputies traitors. In the ensuing hysteria Hitler was able to expel these 81 deputies from the Reichstag and thus secure for himself absolute power. A number of Communists, including the Bulgarian, Dmitroff, and a half-witted Dutchman, Van der Lubbe, were tried for arson and treason—though there is little doubt the Nazis themselves staged the fire. This trial, designed as anti-Communist propaganda, was a complete failure. Dmitroff defended himself and others so ably that all were acquitted with the exception of the wretched Van der Lubbe, who was executed.

1933 NEW LEADERS IN U.S.A. AND GERMANY. At the time, the taking of office of Franklin Delano Roosevelt as President of the United States and the appointment in the same year of Adolf Hitler as Chancellor of Germany appeared to be unrelated. By a twist of fate Roosevelt was to be, twelve years later, one of the principal architects of the Allied effort which led to the death of Hitler and the fall of Germany. Roosevelt, who is above seen making his inaugural speech at Washington, became President at a time when the world economic depression, which was producing appalling conditions even in the United States, was at its height. His "New Deal" policy was the result. In spite of strong opposition his plan received wide approval, and he was re-elected President in 1936, 1940 and 1944. Hitler, shown left greeting President Hindenburg, had in 1932 run unsuccessfully for President, but Hindenburg's death in 1934 left the way clear for him.

248

1934 BRITAIN'S POLITICAL LEADERS. The two leading figures in British politics in the period 1923-37 were Stanley Baldwin (right) and Ramsay MacDonald (seen below with his daughter), both photographed in the garden at Chequers, the Prime Minister's official country residence. Baldwin was Conservative Prime Minister in 1923, 1924 and 1935; MacDonald formed Labour Governments in 1924 and 1929. With the formation of a National Government following the crisis of 1931, Baldwin served as Lord President under MacDonald, offices which they exchanged when a Cabinet re-shuffle took place in 1935. They were very different types of men. Baldwin came from a wealthy industrial family, was educated at Harrow and Cambridge, and in the popular mind was the typical country gentleman characterized by his pigs, pipes and tweeds. MacDonald, son of a farm labourer, was one of the makers of the Labour Party. An associate of Keir Hardie, he was appointed secretary of the Labour Party in 1900.

1934 THE TWO PRINCESSES. When Princess Elizabeth was six the Welsh
people presented her with " the little house with the straw roof "—a scale
reproduction of a typical Welsh cottage—built at Windsor. In this charming picture
Princess Elizabeth explains to Princess Margaret the sundial in the garden which
was attached to the miniature house, part of which is shown in the background.

1934 GRESFORD COLLIERY DISASTER. Periodically, in spite of all precautions, disasters in British coal-mines have reminded the public of the dangers of the miner's calling. In this picture hundreds of relatives and friends wait patiently at the pithead at Gresford, small Denbighshire mining village, where in September 265 miners were entombed—one of the worst of all mining disasters in history.

1934 OPENING OF MERSEY TUNNEL. Until the great tunnel under the Mersey
was opened by King George V the road journey from Liverpool to Birkenhead, the great industrial and shipbuilding town on the opposite side of the Mersey,
amounted to some thirty miles. The tunnel reduced it to less than three. This

picture taken at the opening ceremony shows the Royal car being driven into the Liverpool entrance of the tunnel, which is not only the world's largest circular tunnel (inside diameter 44 ft.), but is also the longest under-water tunnel for road traffic. Four lines of vehicles can be accommodated; pedestrians are excluded.

253

1934 CRIME IN AMERICA. Between 1920 and 1935 the United States suffered from an unprecedented crime wave. One of the principal causes was the passing of Prohibition, which provided opportunities for huge financial profits through illicit liquor-running, or bootlegging, as it was popularly termed. This, together with various forms of blackmail, "protection" rackets and traditional forms of crime on a large scale, attracted many who wanted excitement, self-importance and easy wealth, all of which they sought without regard for life and limb—of others. Most notorious of gang leaders was Al Capone (left), large-scale bootlegger. Though two hundred murders are

254

1934 ASSASSINATION OF A KING. This remarkable picture shows gendarmes and civilians in a Marseilles street rushing forward to seize the assassin, Kalemen. In the back of the car are the dying King Alexander of Yugoslavia and Jean Louis Barthou, French Foreign Minister, who had just welcomed the king on an official visit to France. Kalemen himself was a terrorist, but the web in which he was involved had many strands. Croats, Slovenes and Serbs —sections of the Yugoslav nation—all had reason to object to some aspect of Alexander's authoritarian policy. Of these it is probable that the Croats were behind Kalemen, though both Hungary and Italy may have had something to do with the murder. Kalemen had jumped on to the car's running board and fired through the window, hitting both Alexander and Barthou. The former died almost at once; the latter in hospital after being allowed for some obscure reason to wander about for half an hour in a semi-coma amongst the crowd before being recognized. The incident aroused much suspicion. It was symptomatic of the condition to which France had fallen that even her internal security arrangements could not prevent the assassination of a visiting monarch as he set foot on French soil. This tragic episode was to be followed by the scandals of the Staviskey trials and the disgraceful political imbroglios centring round the Cagoulards.

attributed to him and his gang the best the authorities could do was to gaol him in Alcatraz in 1932 for seven years for income-tax evasion. On his release he retired to comparative respectability on his estate in Florida. He died in 1947. John Dillinger was the criminal of the year in 1934. After serving a nine-years' prison sentence he was released in 1933 and formed a gang of experienced murderers and began large-scale bank-robberies. He was caught and sent for trial for murdering a patrolman. He escaped from prison but was cornered and shot down by G-men. The picture, right, shows Dillinger with his arm affectionately on Prosecuting Attorney's shoulder during a pause in the preliminary hearing.

255

1934 GREAT NAMES IN CRICKET. This year the vice-captain of the Australian visiting side in England was Don Bradman, left, who was the outstanding batsman of the decade. He had already made a world record score of 452 not out at Sydney, and in the test series in England in 1930 he averaged 139, and made a then record test score of 334. Possibly the best fast bowler of all time was Harold Larwood, right, of Nottingham, who in tests against Australia 1932-33 took 33 wickets. He and his bowling were involved in the "body-line" controversy, and so great was the feeling aroused that Larwood was not selected for the 1934 tests. In this year, too, Jack Hobbs retired with a grand total of 197 centuries to his credit —easily a record of its kind. He and Herbert Sutcliffe, an equally great batsman a few years his junior, are seen below going out to bat in a test match at Leeds. They long formed the finest opening pair ever to appear in test cricket.

1935 OVER 300 MILES AN HOUR. Driving his famous "Blue-bird" (above), Malcolm Campbell raised his own world's land speed record of 272 miles an hour to 301. He had made records previously in 1927, 1928, 1931 and 1933, and after 1935, like his friendly rival Segrave before him, he turned to motor-boat racing. Unlike him, Campbell survived all his many record attempts.

1935 DAVIS CUP VICTORY. In 1933 Britain had won the Davis Cup—the premier men's international team trophy in lawn tennis—from France and retained it until 1937, when it went to America. The 1935 team (below, left to right), F. J. Perry, H. W. Austin, Roper Barrett (non-playing captain), G. P. Hughes and C. R. D. Tuckey, defeated the strong American challenge.

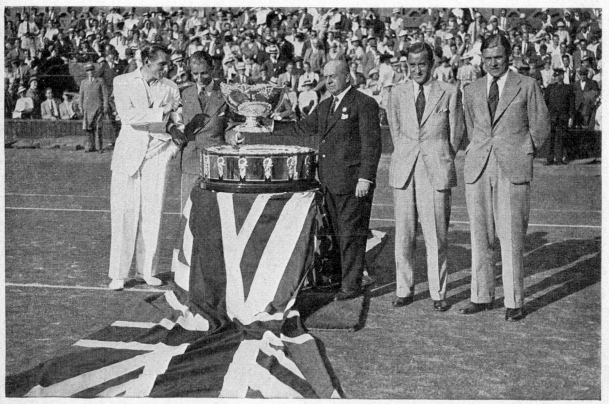

1935 ITALY CONQUERS ABYSSINIA. After considerable preparation for war, Mussolini used a minor frontier incident at Wal Wal as an excuse to attack Abyssinia. Abyssinia appealed to the League of Nations, but the limited sanctions which the League hesitantly imposed had no effect on the course of the war. Using overwhelming forces with the most up-to-date equipment, including poison gas, the Italians found the rough terrain was their principal opponent. The Abyssinians fought gallantly, but they had little equipment and less training. By 1936 Italy had conquered Abyssinia and the impotence of the League to prevent aggression was once more demonstrated. Above, Abyssinian troops are shown on patrol.

1935 MUSSOLINI HARANGUES HIS FOLLOWERS. Grandiloquent speeches, play-acting in uniforms and inflammatory propaganda all prepared the Italian people for imperial adventures. Mussolini had his eye on helpless Abyssinia. Above, he is seen speaking from the balcony in the Piazza Venezia, Rome.

1935 FOURTEEN MILES UP. In a metal ball 9 ft. in diameter, attached to a balloon as tall as a 30-storey skyscraper, two American Army officers reached a record altitude of 74,187 ft. while on a stratosphere flight. The flight began at Rapid City, South Dakota, and they descended (below) 230 miles to the east.

1935 JUBILEE OF KING GEORGE V. Joyful celebrations lasting several days throughout the Commonwealth marked the Silver Jubilee, on 6 May, of the accession of King George V to the throne. In London a thanksgiving service was held at St. Paul's which the King, with Queen Mary and members of his family, and a great representative gathering of the nation, attended in state as shown above.

1936 DEATH OF KING GEORGE V. Less than a year after the Jubilee celebrations the nation was mourning the death, on 20 January, of its sovereign.
Guarded by dismounted Household Cavalrymen and the King's Bodyguard of
Yeomen of the Guard, the King's body lay in state in Westminster Hall, scene of
many famous events in British history, before being taken for burial to Windsor,

1936 WATCH ON THE RHINE. In March, Hitler ordered his troops to reoccupy the demilitarized Rhineland, thus taking the first step not only to defy the terms of the Versailles Treaty, but also of the Locarno Pact. Hitler's confidence that neither the Locarno Pact signatories nor the League of Nations would take any action was justified (it is said that the Germans did not even bother to issue ammunition to the troops who marched in); the desire for peace was too strong in the west, though a resolute stand might have meant Hitler's fall. The silhouetted German sentries above are on the ramparts of an ancient fort overlooking Coblenz.

1936 ABDICATION OF KING EDWARD VIII. A British constitutional crisis reached a climax in December. King Edward, who had succeeded to the throne on the death of his father, had determined to marry an American lady, Mrs. Wallis Simpson. The British people were not at first made aware of the developing constitutional crisis, though the American Press had been speculating about it for some time. Eventually it became impossible longer to maintain secrecy. King Edward's intention was unacceptable to the British and Dominions Governments and on 11 December he abdicated. Right, King Edward VIII and Mrs. Simpson are seen together on holiday in Yugoslavia. He was succeeded by his brother, till then Duke of York, who conferred on him the title of H.R.H. the Duke of Windsor.

1936 "QUEEN MARY" ON TRIALS. Britain's then largest liner, "Queen Mary" (81,000 tons), was completed and sailed on her maiden voyage to New York in 1936. Below, she is seen steaming over the measured mile on her trials off the Isle of Arran. In 1938 she made the fastest crossing of the Atlantic, averaging 31·69 knots.

1936 DESTRUCTION OF THE CRYSTAL PALACE. On a night in November thousands of people from miles around flocked to Sydenham in South London to watch the great fire which destroyed the Crystal Palace. The spectacle was particularly impressive to watchers 10½ miles away on Hampstead Heath, who could see the Palace as a blazing mass on the southern skyline. As this picture

of the smouldering ruins shows, all that was saved was a small part of the main
building and the two towers, all of which were later demolished. Since its erection
at Sydenham in 1852 (see page 36), the Crystal Palace had been a favourite venue
for brass band contests, great choral festivals and shows of all kinds, and the
grounds, with their reconstructions of prehistoric animals, were a popular resort.

1936 SPORTING PERSONALITIES. There were many outstanding figures in the world of sport in the middle of the nineteen-thirties. Notable was the British resurgence in tennis. Dorothy Round won the women's singles at Wimbledon in 1934 and 1937. Right, she is pictured receiving the congratulations of her Polish opponent, Mlle Jedrzejowska (also a great favourite with Wimbledon spectators), after the final in the latter year. Among the men, Fred Perry was outstanding. He won the men's singles three times in succession from 1934. In 1937 he went to America and became a professional. Below, left, Von Cramm (Germany) congratulates Perry on his 1936 victory. At the Berlin Olympic Games in the same year the outstanding athlete was the American, Jesse Owens. He won three events, 100 metres, 200 metres (left) and long jump, in all of which he established Olympic records, and also was a member of a winning

relay team. Henry Cotton was the most notable British golfer of the time, and won the British open championship in 1934, 1937 (below), when part of the match was played in a rainstorm, and, after a long lapse, again in 1948. Widely different as were these six personalities in many respects, they yet had one thing in common. There were then, as now, in big-time sport, many unsavoury "incidents" reflecting little credit upon their central figures. But these six were consistently models of propriety. Cotton, indeed, owes his high reputation among sportsmen of world class as much to his personal qualities as to his golfing skill; and it speaks volumes for Von Cramm and the fair-mindedness of the Wimbledon public that when he appeared in the Men's Singles final in 1937, at a moment of some Anglo-German tension, nine spectators out of ten cheered him on against his redoubtable (and also very sporting) American rival, Don Budge.

1937 CORONATION OF KING GEORGE VI. The coronation of King George VI and Queen Elizabeth took place in Westminster Abbey in May, amid scenes of unparalleled splendour. Celebrations were held throughout the country, even in the smallest hamlets. London itself was brilliantly decorated and the coronation

route was lined with hundreds of thousands of loyal subjects. The above picture, taken in the Abbey, shows the King immediately after the actual crowning, wearing St. Edward's Crown and holding the two sceptres. In front of him is the Archbishop of Canterbury. The Queen, who has not yet been crowned, is seated on the left.

1937 CIVIL WAR IN SPAIN. In 1936 a left-wing government was elected in Spain. For the next five months mob rule prevailed in many parts. Thousands of priests were murdered; criminals were freed. The moderate leftists, such as President Zamora, lost all authority. This was the signal for the organization by the right-wing extremists under General Franco of a rebellion which began in July, 1936. The civil war that resulted was fought with atrocity and brutality by both sides. Germany and Italy backed Franco with men, planes and weapons, while Russia and Mexico helped the legitimate government, despite an international agreement on non-intervention. Weight of arms finally gave Franco victory in early 1939. Above he is seen directing the attack on Madrid. Left, and typical of Republican Spain's resistance, are two of the women defenders of Barcelona.

270

1937 SERIOUS FLOODS IN FENLAND. The Fenland area of East Anglia has always been subject to winter floods despite catchment areas and elaborate drainage. In this year particularly heavy rains fell and the level of all the Fenland rivers rose suddenly and alarmingly. Vast areas were inundated and many outlying farms and even villages were cut off and in some cases submerged. Though no lives were lost material damage was very heavy, as is suggested by this view of the Old West River at Aldreth near Ely. Even more disastrous floods occurred in 1947.

1938 MUNICH. Early in 1938 Hitler absorbed Austria into Germany. Czechoslovakia, half her territory surrounded by Germany, was now in an impossible strategic position. Alleging ill-treatment of those Germans who lived in Czechoslovakia's Sudetenland, Hitler threatened to use force to obtain the cession of these areas. Had the Czechs resisted, both France and Britain would have been involved in war. Britain and France were unprepared for war, and the appeasement mentality gripped their governments and people. War seemed likely when Neville Chamberlain, British Prime Minister, flew to Germany to see Hitler. The resulting Munich agreement, which France and Italy also signed, gave the whole of the Sudetenland to Germany; the Czechs were impotent. There was little surprise that this "last territorial claim" proved but a prelude to the Nazis occupying the now defenceless rump of Czechoslovakia in March, 1939. Above (left to right), Chamberlain, Daladier (France), Hitler, Mussolini and Ciano (Italy) after the signing; below, German armoured forces are seen moving into Prague.

1939 RUSSO-GERMAN PACT. The signing of the German-Soviet Pact in August, 1939, made war a certainty. When Hitler demanded that the Polish Corridor and Danzig should be returned to Germany, Britain and France countered with a territorial guarantee of Poland. At the same time Britain began negotiations with Russia for the military alliance without which the guarantee was worthless. While negotiations were still in progress the world was stunned by the almost incredible news that Germany and Russia had signed a non-aggression pact. Hitler was thus given a clear field against Poland without the fear of a general upheaval in the east and a major war on two fronts. Above, Molotov signs for Russia; behind him, Ribbentrop, Nazi Foreign Minister, seems to be enjoying a joke with Stalin.

1939 CUP FINAL. Football fans had a fine taste of the glorious uncertainty of sport at the cup final at Wembley. All the pundits expected Wolverhampton Wanderers to win, but Portsmouth, playing brilliant football, carried off the cup with a 4-1 win. Left, Jimmy Guthrie, the captain, is chaired off by his team-mates.

1939 WATER SPEED RECORD. From 1932 to 1937 the water speed record was held by Gar Wood (America) who, after a ding-dong battle over two years with Kaye Don (Britain), finally secured the coveted record at 124 m.p.h. In 1937 Malcolm Campbell, fresh from his motor speed-record triumphs, in his motor-boat, also called "Bluebird," raised the record to 128, and the next year to 130. In 1939, with a new "Bluebird" of revolutionary design, he did 141 m.p.h. on Lake Coniston (below).

1939 ROYAL FAMILY VISITS BOYS' CAMP. As Duke of York, King George VI
showed particular interest in youth welfare. In 1921 he founded an annual
camp for four hundred boys, half of whom came from the public schools and the
remainder from industrial areas. This picture shows the King and Queen and the
two Princesses joining in community singing at the last pre-war camp, held at
Abergeldie, near Balmoral. The informality of this occasion is plain to see.

1939 BRITAIN AT WAR AGAIN. Germany invaded Poland on 1 September. British and French ultimatums expired at 11 a.m. on Sunday, 3 September. Britain was at war with Germany again for the second time in twenty-five years. The country braced itself to withstand devastating air attacks from the outset and full air-raid precautions were put into operation. These included the evacuation of women and children from the large cities, and below is seen one of the first groups to leave London. No raids materialized, however, and to civilians the worst of the war was the blackout. Meanwhile, a new B.E.F. was on its way to France, and above an advance unit is seen disembarking. But there was to be no real fighting on the Western Front for many months. Behind the Maginot Line the Allies waited supinely. "Hitler," said Mr. Chamberlain some months later, "has missed the bus."

1939 OVERRUNNING OF POLAND. German armies unleashed a terrifying blitzkrieg against Poland. The Polish Air Force was shot out of the sky and dive-bombers blasted a way for German armoured spearheads against which the masses of Polish cavalry were powerless. After two weeks' fighting western Poland had been overrun and Warsaw was under siege. On 17 September Soviet troops invaded eastern Poland. The war was virtually over. Warsaw endured a terrible air bombardment and held out with epic gallantry until the 27th. Its surrender marked the end of all organized resistance. Above, Polish defenders are seen marching off to captivity through crowds of hopeless and stunned civilians.

1939 BATTLE OF THE ATLANTIC. Even before war was declared, Germany had positioned her naval units to the best advantage for an immediate attack upon Allied, and particularly Britain's, seaborne commerce. If she could only cut off supplies, victory for her was certain. The tactics of the First World War were revived. Unable this time to challenge Britain in a fleet action, Germany relied upon her surface raiders and, above all, her U-boats, to achieve her ends. During 1939, 1940 and 1941 surface raiders were active and often very successful before they were rounded up. Of these, the "Graf Spee," one of the celebrated pocket battleships, was the most notorious shortly after the outbreak of war. Stationed in the South Atlantic, she inflicted serious losses on Allied merchantmen until she was cornered by three British cruisers, H.M.S. "Exeter," "Ajax" and "Achilles," off the River Plate estuary, 13 December, 1939. In a running fight she crippled the "Exeter" but, harried and herself damaged, fled for refuge to Montevideo. Uruguay's government refused sanctuary for more than 72 hours and, rather than let her face another engagement, Hitler ordered her captain to scuttle the ship. Above is seen the blazing wreckage as she settled down. The U-boat menace was far more serious and, as the war developed, nearly brought Britain to her knees. New and improved boats and new techniques (for example, U-boats hunted in packs and co-operated with long-range reconnaissance aircraft) resulted in appalling losses of merchant ships despite the immediate operation of the convoy system. Opposite is shown a typical convoy on its way to Britain. The U-boat menace was at last conquered, and only just in time, by the wide extension of Allied air patrols using radar to detect submarines on the surface. The Schnorkel, which enabled U-boats to remain submerged for days on end, was invented too late to influence the outcome, as it might have done had it appeared earlier.

1940 ATTACK IN THE WEST. The "phoney" war and the long calm on the Western Front were broken with dramatic suddenness in April, 1940, when Hitler invaded Norway and Denmark. The latter could offer only token resistance and was occupied at once. "Fifth columnists" aided the Germans in Norway. Above, a Nazi A.A. spotter watches while troops disembark at Oslo. Britain and France sent an expeditionary force but, except at Narvik, could not hold their positions and evacuated after a few weeks. Even Narvik was abandoned later. The real attack, however, came in May with simultaneous invasion by Hitler of Holland, Belgium and France. Left, German air-borne troops are dropping near a Dutch airfield. Rotterdam was devastated by bombers, and Holland capitulated on 14 May. British and French troops moved into Belgium, but her King, too, capitulated on 28 May after the Germans had overrun the key cities of Brussels and Antwerp.

1940 CHURCHILL BECOMES PRIME MINISTER. Confidence in Mr. Chamberlain and his government was badly shaken by the disasters in Norway. He invited the Labour Party to join him in a coalition but its leaders refused. Following a debate in Parliament, Chamberlain resigned on 10 May and, to the relief of the country, Mr. Churchill formed a coalition government. Above he is seen leaving No. 10 Downing Street shortly after his appointment. Mr. Attlee became Lord Privy Seal and later Deputy Premier; Mr. Chamberlain, Lord President of the Council; Lord Halifax, Foreign Secretary; Mr. Herbert Morrison, Minister of Supply, and Mr. Ernest Bevin was appointed Minister of Labour and National Service.

1940 DUNKIRK AND THE FALL OF FRANCE. The German armoured forces backed by dive-bombers (some of their handiwork is seen left) struck the French defences at the northern end of the Maginot Line. Bursting through the Ardennes on 10 May, they smashed the French IX Army and by the 15th had crossed the Meuse. By the 21st their spearheads had reached the Channel at Boulogne. The British and French troops in Belgium were pinned into a shrinking area on the coast. Only the miracle of Dunkirk saved the British Army, though it lost all its equipment. Below are seen troops waiting to be taken off. The heroic work of the Royal Navy and thousands of volunteers who manned the "little ships," and the gallantry of the R.A.F. fighters combined to bring off a total of over 335,000 Allied troops by 2 June. A marked uplift of

British morale, surprising to foreign observers, was the first result of this escape of an army which had seemed doomed to surrender or destruction. The troops who had been thus rescued, in spite of their humiliating experience, were convinced that, man for man and given up-to-date equipment, they were at least the equal of the victorious Germans. This confidence, which they never afterwards lost, struck the keynote of all Britain's future operations. On 5 June the German forces struck south into a France by now completely demoralized. Italy declared war on 10 June, Paris fell on the 14th, Pétain asked for terms on the 17th and an armistice was signed 22 June, in the same railway carriage and at the same spot in the Forest of Compiègne where Foch had received the German emissaries in 1918. Right, the coach being moved into position.

1940 BATTLE OF BRITAIN. After the fall of France Britain faced Hitler and Mussolini alone. Invasion seemed imminent. But without air control of the skies above the Channel and southern England, Hitler's invasion ships could not move while the Navy kept the seas. The Battle of Britain arose from this fact. It was an attempt to crush the R.A.F., to secure air superiority over England and to demoralize its people. It failed completely. Britain, after Dunkirk, found a new courage. Lacking arms and equipment (lost in France) she enrolled Local Defence Volunteers (later famous as the Home Guard) by the thousand. Some are seen, left, practising their marksmanship. And as the fleets of the Luftwaffe, flushed with continental triumph, rolled over Britain they were met and shot down in hundreds by the fighter pilots of the R.A.F. Below, a

squadron of Hurricanes, followed by Spitfires, are seen on patrol. These two famous single-seater fighters were the only ones Britain possessed which were effective against the German bombers and fighters. They had been put into quantity production only just in time, and, indeed, towards the end of the Battle of Britain the defenders were so short of aircraft that Goering had only to press home his attacks to achieve success. However, Goering, after enduring heavy losses during August and September, switched his raiders from daylight to night-time bombing. London was at first the main target of the night-blitz. A.R.P., extemporized shelters and, above all, London's tube railways (where, as seen right, thousands sheltered every evening) provided the answer. Britain weathered the storm and Hitler was never again to come so near to a final victory.

1940 SECOND GREAT FIRE OF LONDON. His plans for invasion brought to naught by the crushing defeat of his air force in the Battle of Britain, Hitler decided to try to bring Britain to her knees by night-bombing. London, Coventry, Southampton, Portsmouth, Liverpool, Glasgow, Birmingham and many other towns and cities were all badly damaged. At first the raids threatened to overwhelm the inadequate defences and the still-developing A.R.P. organization. But courage, improvisation, improving scientific aids and mounting production of defensive weapons began to master the menace. With few exceptions the civilian

population of the blitzed towns endured their ordeal with stoical heroism. From May, 1941, onwards Hitler was moving his air force to the east for his forthcoming attack on Russia and thereafter raiding was sporadic until 1944. One of the most spectacular raids was the fire raid on the night of 29 December against the City of London. Thousands of incendiary bombs were dropped together with tons of high-explosives. The Cathedral was saved by the heroic efforts of the fire-fighters but acres of buildings were burnt out. This picture shows the height of the raid, St. Paul's stark against the inferno, a fitting symbol of a city's proud defiance.

1941 HITLER INVADES RUSSIA. By the spring of 1941 Hitler was in a dilemma. All western Europe was conquered except for Britain, now too strong to be invaded and which he could not reduce by terror bombing. Moreover, the U.S.A. under the inspired leadership of Roosevelt had carried into law the "Lease-Lend" Act and so ensured for Britain a steadily increasing flood of the sinews of war. The victories of Wavell over the Italians in the Desert and Abyssinia had seriously embarrassed Mussolini, who was further hopelessly involved in a war against Greece. To the east Russia, now in control of eastern Poland, the Baltic States and, after her war against Finland, with much improved northern defensive frontiers, was theoretically a friendly neutral. But everywhere else British sea-power hemmed him in as, some hundred years earlier, it had Napoleon. Hitler's eyes had always brooded over the vast spaces of south-eastern Europe and his decision to break out eastward had been taken as early as December, 1940. Mussolini's plight was an embarrassment which had first to be dealt with. He acted expeditiously and efficiently. Rommel and German forces were sent to rescue the Italians in Cyrenaica, and a lightning campaign overran Yugoslavia, Greece and Crete. Bulgaria, Rumania and Hungary were already his terrified satellites. With his Balkan and Mediterranean flanks secured or repaired Hitler began to regroup his forces. By early June there was assembled in western Poland the most formidable striking force the world had ever seen. Without warning, it was launched against the Russian armies at dawn on 22 June, 1941, on a front reaching from the Baltic to the Black Sea. Of the three main drives, the first in the north towards Leningrad, the second in the centre towards Moscow and the third in the south towards the Ukraine, the second was the most astonishingly successful. Brest-Litovsk fell 23 June; Minsk, 5 July; Smolensk, 17 August; Vyazma, 11 October; Kalinin and Tula, 8 November; and by 6 December Moscow was almost surrounded. In this picture German units are seen crossing the Beresina, in July, against a background of smoke and flame. But despite appalling losses in territory, material and manpower, the Russian armies still fought on, destroying and ravaging their country as they fell back. The German blitzkreig had failed; Hitler had lost the war.

1941 PEARL HARBOUR. Relations between Japan, Britain and U.S.A. had steadily worsened ever since the attack on China in 1937. In July, 1941, Japan seized air and naval bases in Indo-China from Vichy France. In September, 1940, she had signed the Tripartite Pact with Germany and Italy. When General Tojo became premier of Japan in October, war was only a matter of time. But while negotiations were still proceeding in Washington the Japanese struck. On the morning of Sunday, 7 December, carrier-borne planes attacked Pearl Harbour, Hawaii, the chief U.S. naval base in the Pacific. The defences were completely

surprised. Against practically no opposition, Japanese planes first wiped out the grounded American aircraft and then torpedo-bombers attacked the naval craft. Of the eight battleships two were sunk, three completely disabled and the other three put out of action. Several other ships were sunk or damaged, including the destroyer "Shaw" which, as seen here, blew up after being hit. Over 4,000 officers and men were killed or wounded. By this one attack the whole naval balance of power in the Pacific was overthrown. Japan was free to complete her conquest of the Pacific Islands, the Philippines, Malaya, the East Indies and Burma.

1942 SINGAPORE FALLS. Immediately following Pearl Harbour, Japan launched simultaneous attacks against the Philippines and Malaya. After an heroic defence against overwhelming numbers, the last U.S. forces surrendered in the Philippines on 6 May, 1942. In Malaya forces were much more equal, though the Japanese were far stronger in the air. They first overran Siam and attacked south down the peninsula. The British were forced out of one position after another until by 31 January, 1942, they retired into Singapore Island and blew up the causeway. On 8-9 February the Japanese attacked again and by 15 February it was all over, General Percival surrendering with 60,000 troops. Well might Churchill describe the fall of Singapore, the strongest naval base in the Far East, as the "greatest single disaster" in British military history. Right are seen burning ships and docks after a Japanese air raid.

1942 BATTLE OF CORAL SEA. By the end of April the Japanese had overrun the East Indies. In early May they concentrated in the Solomon Islands for an attack on southern New Guinea and later Australia. Warned in time, a U.S. task force attacked with carrier-borne planes and in the Battle of the Coral Sea (4-8 May) inflicted very heavy losses. The U.S. forces were themselves attacked and the carrier "Lexington" was badly damaged. She subsequently caught fire, as seen left, was abandoned and finally sank. The surface forces in this battle, the first check suffered by Japan, never exchanged a shot. In June a similar battle off Midway Island further crippled Japan's naval strength, particularly in carriers. She never was able thereafter to make good her losses.

293

1942 EPIC OF STALINGRAD. Foiled before Leningrad and Moscow in 1941, Hitler made his last bid to smash Russia in the summer of 1942 when his armies crashed into the Caucasus, reaching as far as Grozny. The key to the position was Stalingrad on the Volga and the Germans flung everything into its capture. Above, two Russian soldiers are seen defending a street. From mid-August to mid-November the appalling struggle continued, the bloodiest and most pro-longed battle of the war. The heroic defenders clung on in the rubble to which the city was reduced. Then the Red Army counter-attacked north and south of Stalingrad on 22 November. The German front collapsed. General Von Paulus and his 6th Army, once nearly 300,000 strong, were surrounded. The last remnants finally surrendered on 2 February. By that date other vital places had been recaptured and the Nazi armies were everywhere falling back in a long retreat.

1942-43 VICTORY IN AFRICA. For two years, from July, 1940, the desert campaign in North Africa had swayed backwards and forwards. In May, 1942, the front was a midway position running south from a point on the coast west of Tobruk. Rommel attacked the Eighth Army on 26 May, smashed its armour in a terrific tank battle, captured Tobruk and drove the British back to El Alamein. There he was held. On 23 October Montgomery, heavily reinforced, struck back and won a highly important British victory. Above, tanks are seen moving up during the battle. Before it was over the Allies' long-planned invasion of French North-west Africa (the invasion armada is seen on its way below) was accomplished. German-Italian forces managed to hold Tunis and Rommel fell back to join them. The Eighth Army finally joined up with the Anglo-American forces in Tunis in April, 1943. After fierce fighting the enemy lines were smashed and on 13 May the remnants of their armies surrendered in the Cape Bon peninsula.

1943 FIRST RETURN TO EUROPE. Following victory in North Africa, the
Allies under General Eisenhower prepared for a return to Europe in
Italy, which Mr. Churchill had already aptly styled "the soft under-belly of the
Axis." The strategically important Italian islands, Pantelleria and Lampedusa, were
reduced by aerial and naval bombardment and after some unfortunate delay
through shortage of landing craft the invasion of Sicily, directed and principally
mounted from the heroic island of Malta, was launched on 9-10 July. The airborne
forces, because of unexpected winds and through inexperience, suffered heavily,

but the naval landings on the southern coast made a firm foothold. Above, part of the invasion flotilla is seen off the beaches. The Italo-German forces concentrated their defence in the north-east corner round the Mt. Etna massif, and the Germans at least fought desperately. In fierce battles lasting some six weeks the whole island was cleared with a loss of over 160,000 prisoners to the enemy. The invasion of Italy followed immediately, and these successive blows drove Italy out of the war. Mussolini fell on 24 July and Italy surrendered on 8 September. The Germans had by then, however, taken full control of Italy as far south as Rome and beyond.

1943 FIERCE BATTLES IN THE PACIFIC. Following the naval battles of the Coral Sea and Midway Island the attack on the Japanese area of occupation matured slowly but steadily. In the south-east area General MacArthur began to clear up New Guinea and its neighbourhood. In the Central Pacific Admiral Nimitz attacked the edges of the Japanese conquests. Some of the fiercest and most costly battles of the whole campaign were fought in the Gilbert Islands, almost on the equator. The capture of Tarawa in November (its beach is seen above after the battle) was an epic. From this time onwards Japan was in constant retreat in all theatres.

1944 FALL OF ROME. By November, 1943, the Allies had overrun southern Italy and captured Naples. But the Germans reacted strongly and the terrain, mountainous and cut by rivers, gave them strong defensive positions. Gains were small and costly. Amphibious landings at Anzio were sealed off and the Allies were pinned down. A new attack, launched on 11 May, broke the German front. In a rapid advance the Allies entered Rome (above) on 4 June. Thereafter progress was again slow and costly, the theatre being robbed of troops for France. Not until April, 1945, was the Po Valley entered. Surrender in Italy was signed 2 May.

1944 D-DAY. Plans for a return to France were matured slowly but surely from 1940 onwards. After disappointing delays the Allied forces stormed ashore under massed air cover over the beaches of Normandy on the morning of 6 June. Above, Allied troops are seen later in the day with A.A. guns and barrage balloons already in position. A rapid build-up in the lodgment area was made possible only by the use of artificial harbours (code name "Mulberry") built in sections in Britain and towed across to France. That erected at Arromanches, in the British sector, is seen below. After terrific armoured battles, and aided by saturation raids by heavy bombers, the Allies smashed the German Seventh Army south of the Seine, broke out of the bridgehead and began a race to the Rhine that cleared most of France and Belgium by September. They just failed, most heroically, at Arnhem to secure a Rhine bridgehead and the war dragged on through the winter.

1944 ALLIED AIR POWER. The part played by air power in winning the war against both Germany and Japan cannot be overestimated. By 1942 R.A.F. Bomber Command was pounding Germany heavily in night attacks and by 1943 the U.S. Eighth Air Force in Britain was adding daylight raids. Throughout 1944-45 the crescendo of raids, by heavier and heavier bombers, mounted. The appalling destruction of cities and industrial plant throughout central Europe, and particularly Germany, at the end of the war bore mute witness to the power of the air arm. Similarly, long-range bombers, first from China and later from captured Pacific islands, unleashed an aerial attack on Japan which had brought her to her knees even before the atom bomb was dropped at Hiroshima. It was not only the weight of attack but its range that was so devastating. Above, Liberator bombers of the U.S. Air Force are seen above an oil plant at Ploesti in Rumania during a raid which, as is obvious from the smoke, visibly had already wrought tremendous damage.

1944 FLYING BOMBS ON ENGLAND. By 1943 German scientists had perfected new secret weapons. The first of these, the V.1s, were very fast miniature aeroplanes carrying a heavy war head and driven by a ram-jet motor controlled by a gyroscope. The Germans built numerous launching sites in the Pas de Calais area, but most of them were destroyed by bombing. Some escaped detection and others were improvised. The first flying bomb fell on London 13-14 June, 1944. A round-the-clock blitz began, causing much damage in London and southern England. Of many tragic incidents the destruction (above) of the Guards' Chapel at Wellington Barracks during a service was memorable. The menace was defeated by defensive measures, including a special balloon barrage, elaborate fighter patrols and masses of A.A. guns. V.1s almost ceased when the Pas de Calais area was overrun but by then the V.2, a long-range, high-speed rocket, was being used. The last of these terribly destructive projectiles fell on England in March, 1945.

1945 CAPTURE OF OKINAWA. The conquest in April, after terrific battles, of Okinawa Island (the invasion force is seen above on the beaches) gave the Allies bombing bases within 350 miles of Japan herself. From that moment her fate was sealed. The immense Allied air supremacy was bound to settle the issue.

1945 CAPTURE OF BERLIN. In eighteen months of bitter fighting the Russians drove the Germans from Stalingrad to Berlin, which they entered, as seen below, on 23 April. Some ten days of savage street fighting, together with the effects of terrific Allied bombing and artillery fire, finally reduced the city.

1945 VICTORY IN EUROPE.
In the West the Allies had halted and smashed back Germany's last desperate offensive in the Ardennes by January. In March they forced the Rhine at several points and by April had overrun the Ruhr and driven through Germany to join up with the Russians at Torgau. The German forces were split in two and on 4 May those remaining in Northwest Germany surrendered to Field-Marshal Montgomery at his H.Q. at Luneberg. The emissaries are seen arriving, left. The final unconditional surrender of all German forces was signed at General Eisenhower's H.Q. at Rheims three days later and confirmed in Berlin on 9 May. The triumph had been marred by the death on 12 April of President Roosevelt. The new President, Truman, met Churchill, Attlee and Stalin on 17 July at Potsdam (below) to plan the future of Germany and measures against Japan.

1945 LABOUR VICTORY. The Coalition Government in Britain broke up in June. The results of the election were declared 26 July. Labour won 394 seats, the Conservatives 188 and others 58. Labour had a majority of 148 seats over all other parties combined. Mr. Attlee became Prime Minister and above is seen with members of his Government.

1945 JAPAN SURRENDERS. Her navy destroyed, her forces everywhere overwhelmed, and her mainland under terrible bombardment, Japan put out peace feelers in July; and then the first atom bomb fell on Hiroshima, 6 August. On 8 August, Russia declared war and the next day a second atom bomb fell on Nagasaki. On 14 August Japan accepted the Allies' terms; they were signed by plenipotentiaries (right) on board the U.S.S. "Missouri," 2 September.

305

1946 UNITED NATIONS ORGANIZATION. On 10 January, the 26th anniversary of the birth of the League of Nations, the General Assembly of U.N.O. held its first meeting at Central Hall, Westminster, London. Proceedings were opened by the Chairman, Dr. Zuleta Angel, of Colombia. Clement Attlee, Prime Minister, is seen above welcoming delegates on behalf of His Majesty's Government. Paul-Henri Spaak, Belgium's Foreign Minister, was elected President. The Assembly continued this series of meetings until 13 February. Fifty-one nations attended.

1946 BREAD RATIONING BEGINS. John Strachey, then Minister of Food, announced on 28 June that the Government would introduce bread rationing from 21 July. Normal consumers were to receive 9 oz. per day. This was Britain's first experience of bread rationing throughout history; it continued until 25 July, 1948. Picture below shows a good-humoured first-day rush on a bakery in Commercial Road, part of London's East End.

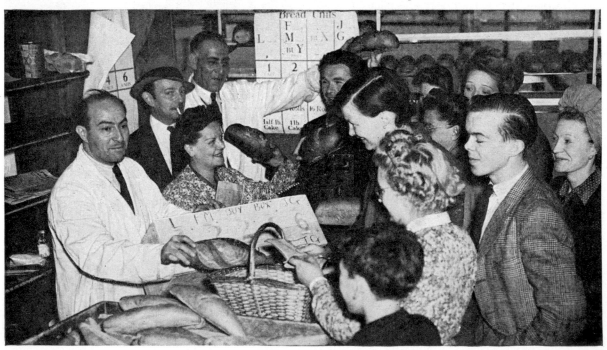

1946 BIKINI ATOM-BOMB TESTS. The second atom-bomb test was carried out
by U.S.A. on 24 July at Bikini Atoll, in the Pacific. The bomb was exploded
under water to test the effect upon ships. A target fleet of over eighty vessels was
assembled. The first effect, pictured above, was a huge mushroom waterspout
which shot up to 5,000 ft. Five ships out of twenty within half a mile of the explosion
were sunk, the rest being badly damaged. This underwater test sank more than
four times the tonnage destroyed in a former test, in which an atom bomb was
exploded 1,000 ft. above the target. Note the relatively small size of the ships.

1947 BRITAIN'S COAL NATIONAL
IZED. Ownership of Britain's
coal was transferred to the State on
1 January under the Coal Industry
Nationalization Act of 1946. The occasion
was marked by a ceremony at the
Ministry of Fuel and Power, but miners,
like these men of Betteshanger Colliery,
Deal, Kent, held their own celebrations.
Some 1,500 collieries, formerly owned by
800 separate concerns, and some 400
of the smaller mines, were nationalized.

1947 ROYAL TOUR OF S. AFRICA.
Their Majesties the King and
Queen, with Princesses Elizabeth and
Margaret, arrived at Cape Town, 17
February, on H.M.S. "Vanguard." In
ensuing months, travelling by rail, road
and air, the Royal party made an extensive
tour, visiting centres in Cape Province,
the Northern Transvaal and Southern
Rhodesia. This informal picture shows the
Royal Family with the late General Smuts
in Natal National Park, where the party
spent a brief week-end during March.

1947 INDIA CELEBRATES INDEPENDENCE. At midnight on 14-15 August the Indian Empire came to an end with the formal transfer of power by Great Britain to the two new Dominions of India and Pakistan. The picture above shows Lord Mountbatten, as the last Viceroy of India, driving in state through New Delhi, accompanied by Lady Mountbatten and Pandit Nehru, India's first Prime Minister. In the lower picture Mr. Rahimtoola, the High Commissioner for Pakistan, is seen addressing the assembly at a ceremony held in London to mark the birth of Pakistan as a new Dominion and the greatest Moslem power in the world. It is also one of the world's largest states in terms of population—the latter being estimated at present as numbering between 90,000,000 and 100,000,000.

1947 PRINCESS ELIZABETH WEDS. Her Royal Highness Princess Elizabeth, elder daughter of Their Majesties the King and Queen, and heiress presumptive to the throne, was married at Westminster Abbey on 20 November to Lieutenant Philip Mountbatten, formerly Prince Philip of Greece. On the preceding day the bridegroom had been knighted by His Majesty and had been created Duke of Edinburgh, with authority to use the prefix "His Royal Highness." The marriage was solemnized before the greatest gathering of foreign Royalty since the coronation in 1937. The picture shows the Royal couple leaving the Abbey.

1948 RECORD BOAT RACE. Always an exciting sporting event, this University Boat Race claimed special headlines. It was the ninety-fourth race, and of the preceding ninety-three Cambridge had won forty-nine and Oxford forty-three, with one dead-heat. The Light Blue crew is here seen establishing a lead at Hammersmith, with tugs and launches following in the wake of the boats, while crowds of excited spectators line the banks or gain a grandstand view from moored lighters. Cambridge made it a jubilee win by 5 lengths and unexpectedly set up a time record of 17 min. 50 sec., thus eclipsing their own 1934 record by 13 sec.

1948 THE MARSHALL PLAN. In June, 1947, Mr. George Marshall, then U.S. Secretary of State, urged European nations to unite in planning their economic recovery. He indicated that any joint reconstruction programme would be backed financially by America. In March, 1948, a sum of 5,300,000,000 dollars was approved by the U.S. Senate, and the picture above shows President Truman discussing European Recovery at Washington with George Marshall, Paul Hoffman and Averell Harriman.

1948 BERLIN AIR LIFT. Following disputes over Allied Control of Berlin, the Soviet Military Government notified U.S., British and French authorities that from 1 April stringent traffic control would be enforced between Western Zones and Berlin. Normal services disrupted, the Western Powers began supplying the city by air. By June, American aircraft were landing at Tempelhof (shown below) every few minutes. The R.A.F. were equally active at Gatow. The blockade, beaten, was lifted on 12 May, 1949.

1948 LAST TRIBUTE TO GANDHI. Called "The Father of the Nation" by Pandit Nehru, and revered by millions, Mahatma Gandhi was shot by a young political assassin in New Delhi on 30 January, on his way to evening prayers. He died within half an hour and his passing caused consternation and grief among followers and admirers throughout the world. Millions lined the five-mile funeral route. His body, draped with the Indian flag, was drawn on an Army truck by detachments of the Indian Army, Navy and Air Force. Circling planes dropped flowers. The picture shows mourners round the funeral pyre beside the Jumna.

1948 NATIONAL HEALTH SCHEME. On 5 July, following prolonged discussions with the medical profession, the new National Health Service came into operation. Scenes like the above glimpse of waiting crowds of out-patients at a Whitechapel hospital were enacted at a large number of places throughout the country.

1948 FOURTEENTH OLYMPIAD AT WEMBLEY. Between 29 July and 14 August a million-and-a-quarter enthusiasts watched athletes from fifty-nine countries compete. Below is seen the impressive closing ceremony. The Olympic flag is held by the Lord Mayor of London, Sir Frederick Wells. Lord Burghley is below.

1948 ROYAL CHRISTENING. Four generations are in this group—Queen Mary, His Majesty the King, Her Royal Highness Princess Elizabeth and H.R.H. Prince Charles. The occasion was the christening of Prince Charles at Buckingham Palace, 16 December. Christened Charles Philip Arthur George, the infant Prince, born 14 November, 1948, is second in succession to the throne.

1949 "AMETHYST'S" HOMECOMING. Enthusiastic scenes took place at Devonport on 1 November, when the First Lord of the Admiralty, the First Sea Lord and other senior Naval Officers welcomed H.M. Frigate "Amethyst" on her return from Far Eastern waters. While taking supplies to the British Embassy in Nanking she had been fired on in the Yangtse by Communist batteries. Crippled and aground, with 17 of her company, including her commander, killed and 20 wounded, she was stranded for months. Then, under Lt.-Cdr. J. S. Kerans, she slipped her moorings one night and escaped. This triumph of daring and navigation, as the First Lord said, "fired the imagination of the free people of the world."

1949 SWEET RATIONING ENDS TEMPORARILY. When on 24 April sweets were derationed, shops everywhere were besieged. Queues like that shown above became commonplace, and shelves which had seemed overstocked were quickly cleared. Among sugar-starved adults were children who had never known the joy of choosing sweets freely. Chaos resulted. One after another the sweetshops began to close their doors, their stocks exhausted. On 14 August sweet rationing was resumed—and sweets reappeared!

1949 BRABAZON'S MAIDEN FLIGHT. Britain's largest civil airliner, 130-ton Brabazon I, built by the Bristol Aeroplane Company, is seen below on her maiden flight on 4 September. She flew for 27 minutes at 160 m.p.h. Begun in October, 1945, Brabazon I is 177 ft. long, with a wing span of 230 ft. Her eight engines, arranged in pairs, give her a range of 5,500 miles. Including construction of a runway involving the demolition of a complete village, the total cost was approximately £12,000,000.

1950 WAR IN KOREA. Following the invasion of South Korea on 25 July by Communist forces of the North Korean régime, the Security Council of the United Nations called immediately for military sanctions against the aggressors. Within two days General Douglas MacArthur's Tokyo G.H.Q. announced that a small advance party was already in Korea and that U.S. air and naval forces of the Far East Command were conducting a combat mission south of the 38th parallel in support of the South Korean Republic. This quickly developed into a full-scale campaign backed by Great Britain and the great majority of the members of the United Nations. For a time advantage lay with the invaders but gradually, as the might of the United Nations force, with its superior air power, made itself felt the tables turned. Above, General MacArthur's own convoy of U.S. jeeps is halted by the roadside near Inchon, where a large-scale surprise landing was made on 15 September—an event which rapidly transformed the situation. Later, the intervention of troops from Communist China again gave cause for anxiety. The size of the knocked-out tanks shows how well-equipped were the enemy.

1950 WEST INDIES WIN TESTS. Cricket was brightened by the visit of the West Indian Test team. Undoubtedly the strongest West Indies side ever to tour Britain, and brilliantly led by John Goddard, it soon proved its mettle for, after losing the first game in the series, it proceeded to win all the others. Above, Gomez is caught by McIntyre in the decisive fourth Test, commenced at the Oval on 16 August, when England was defeated by an innings and 56 runs. In batting, bowling and fielding the visitors surprised everyone and proved themselves clearly the better side.

1950 DEATH OF FIELD-MARSHAL SMUTS. On 11 September, at the age of 80, Jan Christiaan Smuts passed away at his home near Pretoria. He had been ill since May. A great South African and Empire statesman, he had been twice Prime Minister of South Africa—from 1919 to 1924 and from 1939 to 1948. He was given a state funeral with full military honours on 15 September. The picture below shows the cortège passing through the streets of Pretoria. As statesman, soldier and philosopher he enjoyed a unique reputation throughout the entire English-speaking world.

1950 OPENING OF THE NEW HOUSE OF COMMONS. The old House of Commons was destroyed by German bombs in May, 1941, and thereafter Members met for nine years in the Chamber of the House of Lords. In May, 1948, the foundation stone of a new Chamber was laid on the site of the old House. Designed by Sir Giles Gilbert Scott, it preserves the dignity and intimacy of the earlier Chamber. It seats only 437 Members, but there is enlarged accommodation for the Press, overseas representatives and "strangers." To its equipping the Dominions and Colonies generously subscribed. The opening ceremony was performed by the King on 26 October in the Great Hall of Westminster Palace before 1,700 people drawn from the four corners of the Empire and Commonwealth. They included the Speakers of every Dominion and Colonial parliament. The picture above shows part of the new Chamber early on the morning of the opening, with some of the Members who had taken part in the initial rush for seats. At the close of a momentous hundred years this new Chamber stands, as did the old, a symbol of political freedom.

Made and Printed in Great Britain by Odhams (Watford) Ltd., Watford.   S.251.T